Self-Esteem

The Ultimate Guide to Increasing Your Self-Worth and Confidence Using Positive Thinking, Daily Habits, Affirmations, and Mindfulness Meditation

© Copyright 2020

The content contained within this book may not be reproduced, duplicated or transmitted without direct written permission from the author or the publisher.

Under no circumstances will any blame or legal responsibility be held against the publisher, or author, for any damages, reparation, or monetary loss due to the information contained within this book, either directly or indirectly.

Legal Notice:

This book is copyright protected. It is only for personal use. You cannot amend, distribute, sell, use, quote or paraphrase any part, or the content within this book, without the consent of the author or publisher.

Disclaimer Notice:

Please note the information contained within this document is for educational and entertainment purposes only. All effort has been executed to present accurate, up to date, reliable, complete information. No warranties of any kind are declared or implied. Readers acknowledge that the author is not engaging in the rendering of legal, financial, medical or professional advice. The content within this book has been derived from various sources. Please consult a licensed professional before attempting any techniques outlined in this book.

By reading this document, the reader agrees that under no circumstances is the author responsible for any losses, direct or indirect, that are incurred as a result of the use of information contained within this document, including, but not limited to, errors, omissions, or inaccuracies.

Contents

INTRODUCTION 1
CHAPTER 1: WHAT IS SELF-ESTEEM? 3
    THE BENEFITS OF SELF-ESTEEM AND THE PITFALLS OF LACKING 5
    WHAT EFFECTS SELF-ESTEEM? 6
    SIGNS OF LOW SELF-ESTEEM 6
    SIGNS OF HEALTHY SELF-ESTEEM 7
CHAPTER 2: UNDERSTANDING SELF-AWARENESS 10
    INTROSPECTION 11
    SELF-AWARENESS THEORY 13
    DISTRACTION 16
    WHAT ARE WE FEELING? 18
    DEVELOPING SELF-AWARENESS AND HOW WE SABOTAGE OURSELVES 20
CHAPTER 3: CALCULATING YOUR SELF-WORTH 22
    WHAT IS SELF-WORTH? AND WHY IS IT IMPORTANT? 23
    HOW DID WE GET HERE AND WHERE DO WE GO? 25
    THE TRICKY NATURE OF SELF-WORTH 26
    THE SEVEN DOMAINS 29
CHAPTER 4: LEARNING SELF-ACCEPTANCE 31
    WHAT IS SELF-ACCEPTANCE? 32

HOW DO WE CULTIVATE SELF-ACCEPTANCE? 33
ACCEPTANCE ISN'T RESIGNATION 35

CHAPTER 5: TAKING SELF-RESPONSIBILITY 37
WHAT, EXACTLY, IS SELF-RESPONSIBILITY? 38
ARE YOU TAKING SELF-RESPONSIBILITY? 39
WAYS TO FOSTER SELF-RESPONSIBILITY 40

CHAPTER 6: PRACTICING SELF-ASSERTIVENESS 42
THE DOWNSIDE OF BEING NICE 43
WHAT DOES IT MEAN TO BE SELF-ASSERTIVE AND WHY DOES IT MATTER? 44
ASSERTIVENESS VS. AGGRESSION 46
BECOMING MORE SELF-ASSERTIVE 47

CHAPTER 7: SELF-ESTEEM AND POP CULTURE 50
SOCIAL MEDIA REALITY VS. ACTUAL REALITY 51
NEGATIVE EFFECTS OF SOCIAL MEDIA 56
POSITIVE ELEMENTS OF SOCIAL MEDIA 57

CHAPTER 8: START BUILDING YOUR CONFIDENCE 62
HOW TO IMPROVE YOUR CONFIDENCE 63
ACTIONABLE STEPS TOWARDS SELF-CONFIDENCE 66

CHAPTER 9: HOW TO LIVE WITH PURPOSE 68
WHAT IS INVOLVED IN A MEANINGFUL LIFE? 69
BENEFITS OF A PURPOSEFUL LIFE 70

CHAPTER 10: MEDITATION AS A MINDFUL PRACTICE 73
THE SCIENCE OF MEDITATION 74
HOW TO MEDITATE 76
OTHER ADVICE AND CONSIDERATIONS 78

CHAPTER 11: DAILY AFFIRMATIONS 81
SELF-AFFIRMATION THEORY 81
EXAMPLES OF DAILY MANTRAS 82

CHAPTER 12: APPLYING SELF-CARE 85
WAYS TO IMPROVE OUR SELF-CARE 86
THE INTERNAL ELEMENTS OF SELF-CARE 89

CONCLUSION	90
HERE'S ANOTHER BOOK BY MARK JEFFERS THAT YOU MIGHT LIKE	96
REFERENCES	97

Introduction

We often talk or hear about self-esteem, but many of us don't really have a good understanding of what it means, how it is developed, and how one can cultivate it. Psychologists have long been interested in figuring out how and why people develop self-esteem, feelings of self-worth, and how this affects their overall lives and wellbeing. If most of us look closely at our lives, we can see how self-esteem, or a lack of it, has played a profound role in how we become who we are.

There is much evidence to support the notion that people with healthy levels of self-esteem function better in life, reporting higher degrees of personal and work satisfaction than those with lower self-esteem. While there is a lot of evidence suggesting that much of our feelings of self-worth are ingrained in us from our experiences, this doesn't mean we cannot make changes.

This guide discusses what self-esteem is, its importance, and factors that contribute to how we feel about ourselves. Once we have laid this groundwork, we will look at ways you can take control of your life and feel better about yourself and your prospects. It is a long, hard road for many, but the process of self-knowledge is highly rewarding and can have dramatic results in our daily lives.

We look at different ways to take control of our lives, thoughts, and feelings. We talk about the importance of self-awareness and self-acceptance, and taking responsibility for our thoughts and subsequent actions. None of this is easy and will not produce changes overnight, but with conscious effort, one can improve their response to emotional stimuli, learn to love themselves, and to gain more confidence about their abilities and potential in this world.

The advice we present in this book is backed by scientific rigor, and real-world testing, that has shown its effectiveness. Lacking positive self-esteem and feelings of self-worth develop because of experience over time, and thus, one cannot expect that it can be remedied overnight. It will be a long process and one that will probably have setbacks, but the ultimate end is more self-acceptance and self-love that will help you achieve what you want in life and give what you offer to the world.

Chapter 1: What Is Self-Esteem?

We often equate self-esteem with feelings about self-worth and the amount of respect we have for ourselves, including how we treat our bodies and mind. The dictionary defines self-esteem as "confidence in one's own worth or abilities; self-respect." This is a good definition, but the meanings of other words might need to be fleshed out. Confidence refers to how well we think we stack up against other people and how much weight we put behind our own thoughts, feelings, and ideas.

Worth is a bit harder. There are people who know they are good at certain things but still don't feel like they are worthy of respect and love, which many psychologists equate to low self-esteem. Abilities can also be tricky since they don't necessarily correlate with reality, which we will touch on below.

There are incredibly confident and resilient, who considerably overestimate their skill or talent. Finally, self-respect is another term we need to look at a bit more closely.

Many people would link self-respect with feelings of being worthy of love and, well, respect, but when looking at self-respect as it relates to self-esteem, we must look at the action. We can *say* we have self-respect all we want, but if we never concern ourselves with self-care and meeting our basic needs it won't make it true.

Just with the definition alone, we see how tricky it is to pin down what self-esteem is, which is part of what makes psychology, in general, a difficult area of science. So many of these concepts are subjective, and what we report may not coordinate with reality.

At first blush, most of us would probably think we have a healthy level of self-esteem, but upon probing deeper, we find there is a lot about ourselves that we haven't learned how to accept. Subsequently, this can have negative effects on our behavior and our lives.

Many people correlate high self-esteem with success. Although there can be a strong correlation between the two, *correlation does not equal causation*. There may be a relationship between the two, but that doesn't mean that one causes the other. More research needs to be done, and this is a difficult topic to get solid research data on.

Low self-esteem can undoubtedly cause issues. People with low self-esteem are more likely to have poor interpersonal relationships, find their careers lacking, and give themselves improper self-care. It should also be mentioned that excessive levels of self-esteem, what we most often call *arrogance*, can also cause problems. People overconfident to the point of arrogance often have issues with their interpersonal relationships and are prone to conflict. Either extreme is not a good thing. Like with so many things in life, the goal is to find the right balance.

So, it is clear that both low and excessive levels of self-esteem pose problems, meaning we want to fall somewhere in the middle. We need to accept and value ourselves enough we care for our basic needs and know how to ask for what we need in life, but we don't want to take this to such an extreme we see ourselves as more valuable than others and seek to dominate rather than cohabitate with others.

The Benefits of Self-Esteem and the Pitfalls of Lacking

People with low self-esteem often feel like a proverbial "doormat" because people walk all over them, and they feel as if they have little to no control over their lives. For people who lack self-esteem, positive feedback may be hard to handle. We all know that person that, when given a compliment, argues that it isn't true.

Excessive fear of failure is common in people with low self-esteem, and that often means they never try things that could lead to failure, even when it is something the person would love or be very good at. People with low self-esteem often talk about a lot of missed opportunities in their life. Roads are not traveled, and risks are not taken due to fear of failing along the way.

The amount of self-esteem you have can play a dramatic role in the success or lack thereof one's experiences in life. Someone's level of self-esteem can inform the risks they take in their life, the goals they choose to (or not choose to) pursue, such as better education and career opportunities. It can also affect expectations regarding interpersonal relationships.

Healthy levels of self-esteem allow you to see and accept your strengths and your weaknesses. It helps you express yourself to others, tell them how you feel, and know how to ask for what you need. People with healthy levels of self-esteem can take a compliment, but they can also take and grow from negative feedback.

People with adequate self-esteem have a good understanding of their abilities and know when to take risks. Taking risks can help build confidence from the success we see from the risks and what we learn with the failures we will experience along the way.

For many, their sense of self-worth and value is directly tied to self-esteem. If one doesn't feel good about oneself, they likely don't place a ton of value on themselves either. The sad thing is this is often expressed in poor self-care. Self-worth refers to the beliefs you hold about yourself, your abilities, and your value to the world.

Psychologists think of self-worth as a trait largely stable and enduring. That doesn't mean it cannot change, but it does show it is more difficult to break an ingrained trait.

What Effects Self-Esteem?

Abraham Maslow was an influential psychologist who developed a hierarchy of human needs. He theorized that self-esteem could profoundly affect our ability to meet our needs. He posits that both self-respect and respect from others is vital to meeting our needs. We cannot reach self-actualization, the highest level of his hierarchy, without both things.

A lot of things can affect self-esteem, from personal disposition, disability, and even genetics, though much more research needs to be done to understand this potential connection.

Life experience seems to be the most important factor in determining someone's level of self-esteem. People who rarely receive positive feedback or reassurance are more likely to have lower levels of self-esteem.

Signs of Low Self-Esteem

- The feeling that most people are better or more worthy than oneself
- Struggling to say no or to express needs and feelings
- Little to no confidence in one's skills and abilities
- A tendency to look at life negatively
- High levels of feelings of shame, embarrassment, pessimism, and fear of failure
- Feeling the needs of others supersede your own

Signs of Healthy Self-Esteem

- Knowing how to say no and ask for what you need
- The ability to express emotions
- The tendency to look at life positively
- The ability to move on quickly from bad experiences
- Having a healthy, realistic, and positive outlook on one's abilities
- Acceptance of one's own strengths and weaknesses
- The ability to accept both positive and negative feedback

It is easy to see how important healthy levels of self-esteem are in life, but good performance in work or school is not the cause of self-esteem. Self-esteem can be gained from good performance. It is more a determinant for risk one will take to further themselves in life.

As we noted earlier, there is a fine line between having high self-esteem and being overconfident even to the point of narcissism. People with excessive levels of self-esteem may see their lives as only successes, but a closer look at their life often paints a different picture. Overconfidence can easily alienate someone from those around them, and it can be a turn off in intimate relationships. Overconfident people are more likely to experience unnecessary conflict in life.

People with healthy levels of self-esteem make better leaders as they aren't afraid to speak up or be critical, but this skill can also lead to conflict. Not all conflict is a bad thing. Sometimes real problems can be solved with healthy conflict.

People with high levels of self-esteem report high levels of happiness and life satisfaction, whereas people with low self-esteem often report higher levels of anxiety and depression.

Those with high levels of self-esteem are more likely to take the initiative. They are more likely to experiment in life and this can be both good and bad depending on what that experimentation entails.

Self-esteem does not correlate with ability and talent. There are people with very high levels of self-esteem with little to no skill and highly talented people who think poorly of themselves. So inherent talent is not affected by self-esteem, but the success or risk we take with that talent may be.

With just this brief introduction, it is easy to see why self-esteem has long been a big concern and area of interest for people in the social sciences. It can have a profound impact on one's life and what they get from it. There is a debate in the social sciences about the value placed on self-esteem. There are those who think we overvalue it, and others feel like it needs to be the prime focus of research.

America has long been a country that fosters high levels of self-esteem, and data has shown these efforts have been effective. Americans tend to have higher levels of self-esteem than citizens of other countries, but there are a lot of debates about the usefulness of this data. Some say that the wording of the survey questions is leading and may inflate the subsequent data, leading to results that stray from actual reality.

Serious methodological issues make the study of self-esteem difficult and often ambiguous. Most often, self-esteem is measured through self-reporting, which is notoriously unreliable. The way a survey question is worded can also lead, which can affect the responses, and thus, the outcome of the study.

With self-reporting, there are tons of issues. People like to please – and often want to respond to how they feel presents themselves in the best light or that provide the answer the researcher wants to hear. People may answer untruthfully to feel better or to appear more socially acceptable, even if this isn't their inner reality.

This has led to developing more subtle measures harder for respondents to "fake." Measures like the Rosenberg Scale have grown in popularity, as it is a more reliable measure that is less prone to false reporting.

One of the biggest issues with testing for self-esteem is the need for objective measures that aren't affected by cultural and other factors, which is a lot harder than it might seem. This means we are likely to continue to struggle to find universally applicable measures of self-esteem. There is no area of the brain we can scan to get a reliable and unbiased number about the amount of self-esteem a person possesses.

This might lead some to think, "what's the point in studying something so slippery?" and the short answer is because it plays such a huge role in the outcome of people's lives. Self-esteem can affect how well one takes care of their physical and mental needs. It can affect what they choose to pursue or not.

We should close this brief introduction by noting that for many people, self-esteem can be variable depending on the circumstances they are facing in life. There are people who just seem to, innately, have high levels of self-esteem and those whose self-esteem is related to how much they fail or succeed in a given effort. Self-esteem is a much more complicated issue than many originally thought, and that means that high self-esteem is good and low self-esteem is bad is not inherently true.

Chapter 2: Understanding Self-Awareness

The concept of self-awareness also seems obvious at face value. Most would say they are self-aware, but when we look at this idea a little more closely, again, things start to change.

But much of what we do daily is done on autopilot. We have a set routine we are so used to following. Because of this, we do things with little conscious thought given to what we are doing and why. Most of us are unaware of how much of our life is spent this way.

We can think of self-awareness in terms of levels. First, "what am I doing?" Next, "what am I feeling?" And finally, "where are my blind spots?"

Life is obviously better than the alternative, but it isn't always great. We have to deal with failures, irritations, obligations, frustrations, and pain, but the flip side encases positive emotions of love, joy, success, and happiness. The tendency to avoid thinking about or confronting negative emotions is a natural human defense mechanism, but for many of us, this becomes our go-to response for any emotionally stressful or demanding situation. Often, we turn to defense mechanisms as opposed to tackling our feelings head-on.

Introspection

Introspection is a lot like awareness, but it is directly tied to the self and not an external actor or force. It refers to how much and how often we look inward and examine our thoughts, feelings, values.

We are very familiar with observation, which is an external focus on the world, but many of us aren't very familiar with introspection. It plays a key role in our ability to know, understand, and accept ourselves, which is a huge part of developing healthy levels of self-esteem. We rarely spend much time thinking about our mood states in the past and the present, why we feel this way, and what this might tell us about our situation and ourselves. This is something that interests philosophers and psychologists, but we would all do well to have a better understanding of what this means and how to use it.

When we think about learning, particularly about self, we might think of brain wave machine readouts or New Age-type things such as contacting our past lives, but that is missing the point and looking at the extremes.

Not all learning is book learning. Sometimes we have to harness our inner philosopher and just think about thinking. Think about feeling. Think about the source or root of our ideas, values. I can almost see eyes rolling right now as many of us feel like we are way too busy to participate in something like this, but we aren't, and we really should.

While we won't get in the weeds, there is a camp of philosophers that think that self-knowledge is the basis for acquiring any other knowledge, and if we want to have a better understanding of the world around us, it can be helpful to start with ourselves.

In today's world, so many of us are busy, and even when we aren't, we feel it's selfish to spend time on ourselves or think about our thoughts and feelings. We take away from work, from family, from our friends, and from whatever else. While too much introspection makes someone self-absorbed, the opposite isn't good either.

We have to make time for ourselves, mentally; otherwise, we will never understand the root of our behavior, what we are feeling, or why we are feeling that. If we want to take control of our lives and improve self-confidence, we will have to be willing to take a close, deep look within ourselves, no matter how difficult or uncomfortable it might make us.

Introspection might best be understood as a tool that can help develop self-awareness, which we will look at below. Not only is it a tool, but it is also a powerful one that can offer us with a great means to get to know ourselves as we are. But what, exactly, counts?

Well, making a sad face in the mirror and then assuming the emotion you are feeling is sadness is not how to do it. There is a lot of disagreement about what is specifically entailed as a part of the functional process of introspection, but it has to be a process that allows us to develop ideas about ourselves that we can test against different conditions such as thought experiments.

Introspection can only give us insight into our own minds, and nothing we learn from this can be generalized to anyone else. When we introspect, we are thinking about how we are feeling right now and probing more deeply into our thoughts to see what we can learn about ourselves from them.

It requires us to detect or directly acknowledge the mental state we are now in, to give us the basis from which we can analyze it.

Now, let's move on to self-awareness and the psychological theory surrounding it.

Self-Awareness Theory

Self-awareness is more complicated than it might first seem because it refers to more than just knowing and understanding yourself. It also refers to how realistically and accurately you view yourself. This might seem easy to do, but in practice, it proves otherwise.

It is likely impossible for us to find an accurate measure of our self-awareness, and it seems far-fetched that psychology will show us a way to quantify this shortly. But this doesn't mean we can't approximate it through introspection and understanding, which is something everyone should do.

Basically, self-awareness is more akin to degrees than any concrete amount of self-knowledge, but if we never look within and give our thoughts and the credence of our thoughts, we will have a hard time even reaching a healthy self-awareness level.

In 1972, Duval and Wicklund developed *the self-awareness theory*. The basic idea is that, at least in some way, who we are as a self is distinct from what we think and feel. As they said back in the 70s, "we are not our thoughts."

Most of us rarely, if ever, give our inner self much thought. We do so many things on autopilot, and much of our life consists of distractions, which we will look at below in greater detail.

It's not that we can't focus on our inner self; it's that most of us choose not to and live by a routine mindlessly where we rarely never give ourselves any regard. The ability for self-evaluation may be something unique to humankind, but it is a skill we should make more use of, considering it is so helpful in our journey towards healthy self-esteem.

When we do engage in self-evaluation, we often look at our thoughts and actions and measure how closely these come to our stated values and beliefs. This can be uncomfortable as there are times we may not like what we see, but that doesn't mean we need not see it. The more we learn about ourselves, the more we can change our mindset and control our behaviors in ways more in line with our values and beliefs.

In this theory, there are two possible outcomes of our self-evaluation. We either pass or fail. If we pass, it means we have determined that our thoughts and actions are in line with our beliefs and values. If we fail, it means we do not.

But here is where we need to step back. Where do our beliefs and values come from? This question is not as easy to answer as we might think. We pick up many of our beliefs and values from our family, our community, and society. Our values are often culturally based, which means they can vary across cultures.

With beliefs, these, too, are largely derived from our family, where we live, our education.

But what we are likely to find when we practice introspection is that many of our values and beliefs are a lot hollower than we might have thought. Do we even understand why we hold the values we do? What is the evidential basis for our beliefs? Are they even corroborated with evidence, and if so, how does one deal with the cognitive dissonance of discovering one holds *false* beliefs?

We can't provide the answers to these deep questions in a short book, but this little window should go to show just how shaky our internal life often is when we don't give it much thought and regard. Our brain takes mental shortcuts that allow us to continue our autopilot routine, which can cause us to develop what we think are ingrained beliefs not supported by reality.

Our idea of what passing and failing will look like and what standards have to be met will also vary from person to person. So, this is not a very objective measure; but then, it is hard to see how it can be. While it might not stand up to scientific rigor, it does give us a decent understanding of where we think our life is versus where we think it *should be*.

When we find ourselves failing at living by our values and standards, there are only two options. We can adjust our standards so we now meet them, or we can work to change our actions and behavior, so it comes more in line with the things we think, feel, and believe. The other option is to choose distraction and simply not think about it.

If this is what you were going to do, you probably wouldn't be reading this book! So, let's continue on.

We do have control over the standards we place on ourselves, and it isn't necessarily a bad thing to revisit and rethink them. Many of us hold ourselves to a much higher standard than we would anyone else, and obviously, this isn't fair.

We might also have unrealistic expectations for ourselves that, when we invariably fail to meet them, make us feel like we are failures in life that can't live up to our perceived potential. As much as we would like to think we could all be rock stars and football players, we must be honest with ourselves, not kick ourselves and let that negative inner critic take over. Because you, as someone with poor eyesight, could never be an airplane pilot, for instance. That just isn't a reasonable expectation for us to hold for ourselves.

In our evaluation, we might also find we are placing way too much emphasis on a successful outcome and not enough on our *performance*. The amount of effort we put into something is a thing we need to pat ourselves on the back for, regardless of how it turned out. A good performance is a good performance, regardless of the results. A lesson we will see repeatedly in this book is that we must cut ourselves some slack.

Developing a good sense of self-awareness helps us to become more proactive and is likely to boost the confidence we have in our thoughts and abilities because we have consciously considered them, rather than simply making assumptions about ourselves.

The more aware we are of ourselves, the more in control of our actions and feelings we become. While we won't be able to stop from feeling a certain way, with time and effort, we can understand why we react a certain way to a given situation. If this reaction is negative, ways we can exhibit more self-control, so these feelings don't cause issues in our life.

Psychologists Ridley, Schultz, Glanz, and Weinstein found in 1992 research that people with a good degree of self-awareness also tend to make better decisions for themselves and their lives. This shouldn't be too surprising as the more we know and understand about something, the better our assumptions and ideas about it will be, even when that something is ourselves.

Distraction

For many of us, distraction is our response to bad news and negative emotions. It allows us to move on without having to face the issue that may prove uncomfortable or difficult, but distraction is also a good thing. It is a healthy reaction since it wouldn't be good for our physical or mental well-being if we could never let go of life's problems and lose ourselves in something mundane.

Distraction is a healthy defense mechanism that allows us to deal with unavoidable stresses, but the problem arises when distraction is our only response to stress or negative issues. Our refusal to face a negative reality can cause more problems than it is worth.

Not that one should avoid distraction; as we noted above, it is a useful and healthy way of dealing with reality. It can be vital for our mental and physical health. The key is to be aware of distractions and when we use them. Distraction can also become autopilot, like so many other parts of life.

Are you in control of your distractions, or are you simply on autopilot? The goal is to be more in control of our use of distractions so we can be more discerning about when to employ them. We should consciously choose distractions rather than mindlessly engage in it. You must pay attention to yourself, and what you are doing so you know when you are "checking out" of reality and how long you did this.

Distraction is everywhere, from scrolling through social media to daydreaming. We often do this with little awareness of the fact that we are doing this. Do you know how you are using your time? When we pay attention to what we do, we often find that a lot more of our life is spent on distractions we had originally assumed. As we pay more attention to our actions and what we are doing with our time, we can take more control of our life.

This is also important with interpersonal relationships. We often think we are more present and better listeners than we are. This can have an impact on the quality of our relationships. Sometimes our distractions are causing us to disconnect or alienate those around us, and we may not even know this is happening.

Again, it is important to say that we don't recommend eliminating distractions. They are fun and often a useful part of our lives that gives it meaning and value. We just need to become cognizant of when we are employing distraction, how long we are doing it, and can pull ourselves out when we realize we are using it at the wrong time.

It is easy to distract ourselves to where it becomes routine - we want to avoid this and correct that tendency. When you notice you've checked out, don't simply snap back to reality. Consider the surrounding situation. Do you do this at work? Around family and friends? Consider what it is about these situations causes you to reach for distraction.

We must be able to look at these situations objectively and without judgment. Otherwise, we cannot address what is causing us to turn to distraction rather than be present in that moment. For example, say I wear headphones everywhere I go. If I think about it on the surface, I might just think I enjoy listening to music. While this is certainly true, what is the reason I reach for my earbuds any time I'm in public? For me, it is a defense mechanism against social interaction – a fear of people.

What Are We Feeling?

So we can see how we use distraction, almost without notice, to avoid being present and aware of our lives and what is going on in and around them, but it isn't enough to just know what you are doing; it is also important to understand what you are feeling.

We often feel emotions, even intense ones, but don't know how to find or pinpoint what exactly it is we are feeling and why. It's hard to pinpoint the source of emotions if you don't even know what it is you are feeling at a given moment.

Reducing and controlling distractions, as we talked about in the previous section, means we will be more present in our lives and thus must deal with emotions. This can be uncomfortable and confusing, especially at first. Many people avoid and don't like thinking about their emotions because it just feels so big and overwhelming. The more intensely we feel them, the less we want to face them, it seems.

When you come face-to-face with your emotions, you discover your true self and how you feel about things in life. Learning about self will be inherently uncomfortable, largely, because it is something we seem to disregard.

As we talked about above, learning and controlling distraction isn't nearly as personal or emotionally rife as figuring out what and why we are feeling this way. Often, people have a much easier time with that than developing self-awareness.

It is likely to take a long time to understand what you are feeling and the possible sources of a emotion. Many people spend years in therapy trying to figure out their emotions and the source of feelings so deeply felt. Also, to make things more difficult, emotions are ever present and often have no profound meaning or source. Sometimes we are happy because we saw something cute and for no other more profound reason than that. Over time and with reflection, you can separate feelings that need to be probed and addressed from random feelings that are simply the result of being human.

Here's where things get even more confusing. Human emotions can, in themselves, be distractions. For example, I might mire myself in an endless stream of cute kitten videos so I can feel happy even when my life is falling apart around me. I am using the kittens as a happiness distraction, so I need not address real issues in my life.

Examining emotions will, naturally, lead to other emotions, causing us to delve into an endless spiral of self-reflection. We always want to peel back one more layer of the proverbial onion to see what's underneath, but there comes a point where it becomes counterproductive to our efforts.

Experts recommend going just a few layers down into our emotions and being content with what we learn. Otherwise, we will end up in an unhealthy loop of self-inquiry.

We must also address our blind spots if we wish to become more self-aware. All this self-reflection may make you realize how empty and hollow many of our thoughts and opinions are. So much of our life is spent reacting to how we feel at a moment rather than acting consciously and with forethought. We aren't as deliberate or rational as we would like to think, and emotion directs our behavior a lot more than we realize.

The mind is a finicky thing and has a lot of blind spots that are helpful to understand. Memory is inherently unreliable. We overestimate how much we really know about a subject and often even our abilities. We don't always change our minds in the face of conflicting evidence; some of us may even double down. We focus on things that mesh with our view of reality and ignore those that might make us rethink our beliefs.

While these may seem like (and can be) serious issues we can do little about, being aware of them is part and parcel of self-awareness. It is understanding the inherent issues all humans deal with. We must accept them during this process of self-discovery, becoming more self-aware that our beliefs and values are often weaker and less backed by evidence than we may have thought.

We need to learn our patterns of behavior and action so we can put the brakes on negative responses or inappropriate uses of distraction. We also must be realistic about how much we can do to counter the natural pitfalls we all deal with. Being aware of it won't stop them but it is useful in helping us understand others and ourselves.

Developing Self-Awareness and How We Sabotage Ourselves

While a lot of self-awareness is accepting things about ourselves that we cannot change, there are a lot of ways we can foster self-awareness. Mindfulness, or being present and closely observing one's emotional and physical state, is an useful way to gain more self-awareness. Mediation can also be helpful and can be used with other mindfulness strategies. We will discuss meditation in more detail in a later chapter.

Keeping a journal or diary is also a great way to foster self-awareness. Putting something into words requires us to look more closely at our emotions. Talking to others is also useful, and accepting the feedback they can give you - whether it is positive or negative. These things are done in pursuing self-awareness and the greater goal of self-acceptance.

We can do many things to improve the way we see the world and our responses to it that will help foster greater self-esteem, more happiness, and a sense of purpose in our lives. Then, by doing these things, we also become more empathetic with others, and ourselves, which is also a huge benefit.

Seeing ourselves more clearly allows us to better gauge our skill and ability, which can make it easier to decide when it makes sense to take the risk. It can lead to more confidence and an outpouring of creativity. Self-awareness can also help us improve our communication with others, which can enhance interpersonal relationships.

We can just as easily sabotage our efforts as we can benefit from new knowledge and understanding. Self-doubt is a huge killer. It will keep us from even trying due to fear of failure. To a certain extent, doubt is a good thing, as it makes us seek outside opinions, question ourselves, and become more accepting of the change. But excessive levels of doubt cripple us and keep up from taking risks and trying new things.

We shouldn't fear doubt, as it can be helpful, but we need to learn how to control and harness it, so it doesn't run our lives. Having excessive doubt will make us less likely to express our emotions and needs, as we are unsure of ourselves. It can even cause us to lose control over our lives, letting others guide our lives and make our decisions for us.

Chapter 3: Calculating Your Self-Worth

Our feelings of self-worth are often closely tied to self-esteem, which makes perfect sense. Self-worth refers to how we feel about our inherent value, how we stack up against others, and how deserving we are of success and/or happiness. For those with low self-esteem, our sense of self-worth is also often lacking.

People with low self-worth often think that others are more deserving of happiness and success than they are. This can become a self-fulfilling prophecy because if we feel this way we are less likely to take risks or initiatives that could lead us closer to our goals in life.

For all our concern about self-love and valuing the inherent worth of human life, there often isn't a lot of actionable advice on how to foster a sense of self-worth. There are quite a few things that have proven to be highly successful at fostering self-worth, such as daily mantras (we will talk about this in a later chapter) or concern and well wishes from others. But how can we internalize feelings of self-worth so we believe in our worth and value?

Here, we want to look at how to better manage life and its stresses and to develop a better understanding of ourselves that allows us to grow and progress. While their heart may be in the right place, the "you're doing great, sweetie" and "it will all be okay" platitudes don't provide any actual help.

What is Self-Worth? And Why is it Important?

The short definition of self-worth simply refers to the value you place on yourself, especially compared with the value you place on other people. It is an important part of self-esteem, and while it might not be clear at first, having unhealthy feelings about your own self-worth can have a hugely detrimental effect on your life and wellbeing.

People who don't feel like they have value are often unsure of themselves, their thoughts, and their opinions. They aren't likely to speak up when someone says something they don't agree with or something that hurts their feelings.

So, we are less likely to stand up for ourselves when we have low self-worth, and we are also less likely to take risks and make changes that might make our lives better, such as obtaining an education or even getting out of a bad relationship.

Just as important, people who lack self-worth are not nearly as likely to engage in self-care. This means they ignore their physical, mental, and emotional needs, which, in turn, may lead to even worse self-confidence and more.

While it might not be obvious at first, our emotional state can be directly related to the value we place on ourselves. The way we handle stress. How we approach emotionally charged situations and more. Perhaps now it is becoming clearer just how negative feelings of self-worth can dramatically affect our daily lives, our overall health and our wellbeing.

There are psychological theories about self-worth that relate one's feelings of personal value through competition with others. In this theory, the value we place on ourselves is directly related to how we think we stack up against other people.

In today's world of celebrity culture and social media, this can have a profoundly negative impact on our feelings of self-worth. We will touch on this in greater detail below, but suffice to say that we most often engage in *upward comparison*. We compare ourselves with the most successful, beautiful, etc., and thus, are not nearly as likely to feel we stack up like if we compared ourselves with our peers or even ourselves, for instance.

People commonly measure their self-worth based on the upward comparison, but we also measure it based on how we feel we stack up against people we know. Some of us also place value based on the type of people we know. How many important people are in your social circle? For some, this might have a huge impact on how we feel about ourselves.

The way we look and feel is another key factor we use to determine our own self-worth. If we feel like everyone else is more attractive and more stable than us, we are less likely to feel as if we have as much value as those around us.

Our occupation or what we do for a living can also affect how we feel we stack up against others. If we feel like we have an important or "good" job, we are likely to feel more worthy than how someone in a "dead-end job" feels about himself or herself. We will discuss the pitfalls of place personal value on career accomplishments later.

We might also measure our value based on our material success and the stuff we have. If we have a nice house with tons of toys and gadgets, we may feel more worthy and valuable than someone living in a trailer park, struggling from paycheck to paycheck. We will talk about how these factors should do not pertain to how we feel about our worth to society, but the fact is that many of us use this as our guidepost.

How Did We Get Here and Where Do We Go?

Far too many of us are "broken" or "damaged" from negative or traumatic life experiences. Perhaps we have seen a lot of loss in our lives, had unstable family situations or were mistreated or neglected. With all this in mind, it is easy to see why so many of us have a hard time calculating our value and improving our sense of self-worth.

There are several definitions of self-worth, but many relate to life success and how well you have kept to the goals you set for yourself. This might not be the best measure of self-worth since there are plenty of people with a great amount of skill, talent, and work ethic who struggle in life for reasons outside of their control. The main problem with this idea of self-worth is that accomplishments don't make someone more valuable than anyone else - all humans are valuable, and this should be nurtured and fostered in all of us, regardless of our material success.

Self-worth and self-love don't mean just constantly telling yourself that you are great. This might be part of it, but the real goal is to take care of you - physically, mentally, and spiritually. It means learning about and accepting your strengths, weaknesses, and quirks. It is learning to accept that you aren't perfect and that it's okay - nobody is perfect.

There are many reasons it can be difficult for someone to acknowledge their self-worth. Some of us grow up in unhealthy environments that lack love and positive feedback. Others grew up in the shadow of someone they could never hope to "keep up with" in terms of achievement. Perhaps you had parents with a bad relationship, who treated each other poorly, and this was your only source of knowledge and guidance.

Any – or all – of these things can contribute to negative feelings of self-worth. It can make it hard for us to see and accept our own value as humans, but we will say it again, and again, it is there. All humans are inherently worthy and valuable. A lack of self-worth can affect one's daily life.

It can make it more difficult for us to have happy and successful interpersonal relationships and careers. If we don't see our value, we are more likely to accept mistreatment or mediocrity in life. These things can then reduce our feelings of self-worth even more and become yet another vicious cycle.

There is no step-by-step process for developing better feelings of self-worth. It is hard and can be a long process, but the main thing we will need to do is that adage from the Oracle at Delphi: know thyself. We need to learn how to have self-compassion, accept responsibility for our lives, accept our weaknesses besides our strengths, and know that the biggest impediment to our happiness is often us.

People in your life may be contributing to your lack of feeling of self-worth. Perhaps someone constantly criticizes you and has nothing nice to say. This is not helpful to the journey we are trying to take, and it might be a good idea to reduce the influence this person has over your life or cut them out entirely.

You need to take care of yourself, physically and mentally. Evaluating how you use your time, such as how you use and react to social media, can also really help us have a more positive sense of self-worth. We will discuss social media and celebrity culture and how this relates to our self-esteem in a later chapter.

The Tricky Nature of Self-Worth

Like our self-esteem, our feeling of self-worth can be variable with time and circumstance. Our self-worth isn't something many of us think about often or deeply. Sure, we might feel like we have value, but then we reach a stumbling block or experience failure. Then, our feelings of worth and value take a big hit. We rarely see how much of an impact this can have on our lives.

Many people measure their self-worth based on how they stack up against others. This might be in terms of looks, money, career success. These things can affect how we think about ourselves and how we feel like we stack up in society. Though these things have their importance, all people have inherent worth and value, even if they "contribute little" in the classical sense to society.

The measuring stick should be yourself, not your social betters. Look at where you've come from, know who you are, and it will help you come to terms with and accept whom you are. This doesn't mean you shouldn't try to change or improve the things in your life you have control over. Although, it does mean there are elements of your personality that are constant, regardless of outside factors and life experience. These are the things we need to accept as they are.

Learning to cultivate your sense of self-worth will help you come to believe that, as a human, you are enough and deserve love and respect.

In psychology, the self-worth theory posits that our main goal in life is the search for self-acceptance. Many achieve this through material and career success, through competition with others, and through relationships and personal connections. Too many, we calculate our self-worth through constant effort and competition.

The main elements of this theory include ability, effort, performance, and self-worth. It is easy to see how the first three elements might have a determining effect on the fourth. Your abilities (or how you perceive them) are likely to affect your level of effort, which will affect your performance, leading to a self-perpetuating cycle.

The main problem with this theory is that the emphasis is placed on accomplishment, which need not be tied to self-worth. Though this shouldn't be the case, most of us evaluate our self-worth based on effort and accomplishment and how we compare to others.

But achieving goals is great, but your ability or inability to achieve these goals does not reduce your worth. Having a prestigious job isn't a measure of worth; the important part is that you are fulfilled by what you do. A social media following does not define worth, nor do the relationships you do or don't have. Getting older doesn't make you less worthy or valuable, either, despite the value we place on youth in our society.

It is easier to fix your sense of self-worth as a younger person, but that choice has long passed for most of us. First, we must look at things that contribute to our self-worth and learn to internalize this. Identify your inner critic quick to negativity and constantly focuses on failure. It's important to be able to criticize ourselves so we make better decisions, but too often, that negative inner critic is the driving force of how we feel about ourselves, and *that voice isn't always right.*

When you notice that inner critic coming to the fore, step back and think about what that critic is saying. Is it correct? Does it help you to become better? If it is and will, listen to it. If not, ignore it or argue with it. Challenge the voice when it is unnecessarily critical.

To form and maintain mutually beneficial relationships, we need to a positive sense of self-worth lest we end up with someone who dominates or constantly criticizes us and ultimately makes us feel even worse about ourselves. We must be able to communicate effectively. Being loved is not what makes us worthy of love; we are worthy of that inherently. Our intimate relationships should be partnerships; they are not our saviors.

Loving and accepting ourselves makes it easier to love and accept others. It will help us have better interpersonal relationships with family, friends, coworkers, etc.

Self-worth should never be tied to something outside of you. You still have value and worth even if you lose your job or fail to obtain that promotion. Jobs can be transient, and to base our entire sense of self and personal value on something transient is dangerous.

Many psychologists use something called the self-worth scale to allow people to see how they value themselves. Called the Contingencies of Self-Worth, this scale was developed by Crocker, Luhtanen, Cooper, and Bourvrette in 2003. The scale consists of 35 items that evaluate self-worth based on seven "domains."

The Seven Domains

- Approval from others (do we care about what others think about us?)

- Physical appearance (how do we feel like we stack up looks wise?)

- Outdoing others in the competition (how much do we derive worth from doing better than our peers?)

- Academic competence (do we base our self-worth on academic achievement?)

- Family and support (do we need support from family and friends to feel worthy?)

- Being virtuous and moral (do we derive our worth from our acts?)

- God's love (do we have only value if God loves us?)

The scale is rated from 1 (strongly disagree) to 7 (strongly agree). The total number is summed and divided by 5 to get a subscale score. This scale has shown to be accurate and useful to people studying self-worth.

There are many exercises online, including interactive lessons and worksheets, that you can use to help you determine your current feelings of self-worth and to improve them by building up your confidence. These can be very helpful for people who need guidance or are unsure of where to start.

More research needs to be done, just like all other self-esteem research areas, but what we know shows how important it is for our very quality of life to have a healthy level of feelings of self-worth.

Chapter 4: Learning Self-Acceptance

Acceptance is one of those things that seem simple on their surface but prove difficult in action. Most of us have a much easier time accepting and forgiving others than we do ourselves. We tend to be much harder on ourselves than we are on those around us. You don't achieve self-acceptance, and then - boom - you're done, and you have it for life. Rather, it is something that you will probably have to work hard on and perhaps even in perpetuity.

For some, a small setback can make it difficult to look inwardly with love and compassion. All we see is that we made mistakes, we don't look at the struggles we faced or what we overcame; all we see is the result. But life will include failure, it will happen, and that's okay. It doesn't mean we are lesser people who don't deserve love or respect.

So, while many struggle with it, self-acceptance is something we can cultivate with effort, and we will be better and happier people for our effort, even when it's hard.

What Is Self-Acceptance?

Self-acceptance is one term that seems self-evident; however, it may not be as clear as it initially seems. We all want to accept and love ourselves for who we are, which is easier said than done. But with acceptance, what about the parts we don't like or those we wish we could change about ourselves?

The inability to accept negative things or weaknesses about us that are outside of our control to change is a huge impediment to self-acceptance. It is one thing to accept the good things about ourselves, our strengths and attributes, that we feel make us valuable to society, but self-acceptance isn't just about the things we are proud of.

We are humans. All humans are imperfect, and even the person with the highest amount of self-esteem is likely to have a thing or two about themselves that they wish they could change but cannot. The real struggle here is to accept those things too.

There is a lot about who we are that we have control over and can change. On the flip side, there are parts of our personality incredibly difficult or impossible to change. For example, say I am super sensitive. There really isn't much I can do about this, as the feelings and emotions come whether I want them to or not. I may not like this part of myself, but I might not have the ability to change this. Self-acceptance doesn't mean liking these things about yourself, but accepting that they are what they are.

For things like meditation and mindfulness practice, which we look at in more detail below, to have a positive impact, we need to accept ourselves for who and what we are.

It might sound strange, but there is also evidence that lacking self-acceptance can make your experience of certain illnesses or health conditions worse.

It appears there are even differences in the structure of the brain of people who lack self-acceptance. The part of the brain that controls emotions and stress has less gray matter in people with low-self acceptance than those with high self-acceptance. There may also be a lack of gray matter in the areas responsible for controlling stress and anxiety.

An impediment like this might seem all but impossible to overcome, but we can change this. The brain is a complicated and sophisticated organ, and the "paths" we wear in our brain become ingrained, so that is the path our neurons are most likely to follow, but this doesn't mean we cannot create new paths. It takes time and conscious effort, but it is possible.

How Do We Cultivate Self-Acceptance?

We must go into self-acceptance with an open heart and mind. This may require us to change our way of thinking about our circumstances and ourselves and to leave blame behind. We must let go of our feelings of shame and doubt and to open ourselves to positive feelings that move beyond the things that hold us back.

We must move beyond self-hatred and inner criticism. These things do nothing other than holding us back and dislike ourselves for things beyond our control or that we cannot change.

We need to celebrate our strengths, and yes, we all have them, even if they seem useless or inconsequential. Say you are a good knitter. This might seem like it isn't that important, but it is considered a strength that not everyone can do. Count it as a strength that is just as important as career success. Ask yourself questions: Am I kind? Am I good at activity "x"? Do I have a real skill for a hobby? These things are invaluable strengths you should note and be proud of. Think about obstacles or hardships you have overcome. These, too, are strengths.

You will need to consider your social circle. What type of people do you have in your social circle, and why are they a part of your life? Part of self-acceptance might also mean accepting there can be people that are toxic and keep you from being your best self. Consider letting them go or reducing their influence on your life.

Create your support network because we do get to choose our friends. We might not have control over who makes up our family, but we control how much influence we let them have on our lives. We have a lot more control with our friends. Our social circle should be compromised of people who have mutually beneficial relationships. We should uplift our friends, and they should uplift us; real friendship isn't a competition.

Just like you should love and respect your friends, you should have the expectation they will love and respect you.

Self-acceptance will require you to forgive yourself. We have all done things we aren't proud of or regret. We can learn from these mistakes and try to live a better life, and that is how we should take these things. For too many of us, we never forgive ourselves or let go of these failures. We carry around shame and regret over things we cannot change, which hinders our forward progress.

You must be able to forgive yourself and realize that you are not the sum of your mistakes. We learn and grow from our errors and then move on.

Another part of self-acceptance that is related to forgiving ourselves is learning how to shut our inner critic up when it isn't helpful.

It is also okay to mourn our dreams and things unrealized. There is no shame in being upset or regretful about the road you didn't travel. When we were kids, we had such idealized dreams of our future, and most of us don't get there. This is life, but it is okay to be sad about what could have been, but don't get mired in it. Allow yourself to feel sad but then move on, don't get mired in what could have, would have, or should have been.

No matter what your station in life, you can do good deeds, whether it is to donate money or volunteer your time. Helping others allows us to use our time and resources for the greater good. Not only will this make you feel good and do something great for society, but it will also make it easier to argue with that inner critic about your value. It is hard to argue that you are a bad person with no value if you spend your time working for the good of other people.

Acceptance Isn't Resignation

Accepting yourself for who you are, including the mistakes you may have made in the past, is not resignation. This doesn't mean you are burying the notion that you can change or become a better person. Rather, it is simply acknowledging where and who you are at this point in your life.

Whether acceptance stops at this awareness or motivates them to move forward towards a greater goal is up to the individual.

It makes sense to focus our energy on things we have control over. Say you have "two left feet." This means you will never be a star athlete, but that doesn't mean you can't pursue the sport you love with friends or as part of a community effort. It is an effort of rethinking our goals based on our current status and actual abilities.

When trying to learn to love and accept yourself, try to speak to the best you—the self-actualized, best possible version of yourself. Consider what you might do or say in a given situation and give it a listen or even a try.

None of us will ever be completely happy with our lives or ourselves. We are all human, and we need to be accepting and mindful of this. Work hard to stop cutting yourself down or undercutting your potential. You need to be realistic about what it is possible to achieve and make goals based on your actual abilities.

Being kind to yourself is not selfish; it is a basic part of self-care that too many of us neglect. It is vital to living a happy and fulfilled life. While we may not see it, failure and setbacks are part of being humans, and even the most successful person in life experiences this. Love you, flaws and all, and work to change elements of your personality and life you have control over. So, for example, you can't help being upset by something, but you can help how you react or respond to it.

If asked, most of us would say we are okay with who we are and what we have become, but deeper probing shows how untrue this is. Most of us have issues in our own life, unlikeable things about ourselves or regrets we haven't accepted. This is natural, and the problem lies not with the fact that we have regrets or things about ourselves that we don't like, but our refusal to accept these things.

This probing, while uncomfortable, is important to self-knowledge and, ultimately, self-acceptance. Carl Rogers, one of the first psychologists to discuss the importance of positive self-regard, focused on the importance of positive self-regard on our overall mental health and happiness. We must be open to others and can think positively about ourselves. This, Rogers thought, helped us function in the world and in turn, helped us get over negative thoughts and experiences more quickly. He believed that negativity acts as a destructive force that will cause negative issues in life if unaddressed.

Chapter 5: Taking Self-Responsibility

When most of us think of the word "responsibility," we think of the obligations we have in our lives, such as our careers or our children, but it has a slightly different meaning in the psychological community we will need to unpack.

Think about the question, "do you own your life?" Most of us would immediately respond, "yes, of course," but how true is that, really? Just like with self-acceptance, it isn't always true that we own our lives upon closer inspection. For many of us, we are owned by our jobs or the roles we play in society. While this is common, it can also stand in the way of living a happy and meaningful life.

Responsibility naturally makes us think about the obligations or consequences of our actions, which is part of what the word means, but with relation to ourselves, it is a bit more nuanced. Basically, it is a form of acceptance that allows us to take more control over our own lives (or let other entities take control).

Basically, self-responsibility refers to understanding that our thoughts, emotions, and behaviors are our own and impact our life experience. Yes there are outside factors at play, but this remains true on the day-to-day level.

To have healthy self-esteem and live your best life, understand that you, your thoughts, and your actions are responsible for much of your external experience.

How often do we blame others or outside circumstances for the state of our lives? It is far easier to do this than to look inward to see where you contributed and to make changes.

What, Exactly, is Self-Responsibility?

In psychology, *self-responsibility* is also often called *personal responsibility*. This refers to the amount of accountability we feel or place on ourselves for our actions and feelings. This might seem like a fairly new concept, but it has ancient roots, though what it means to be personally responsible, of course, changes with time and place.

The concept of self-responsibility works on the assumption that as individuals, we have some degree of personal autonomy that allows us to decide and act in our lives in response to circumstances or stimuli surrounding us. This is, inherently, not a deterministic viewpoint. It holds we have free will, and along with that comes the responsibility and accountability for the things we say and do.

And this concept presupposes that we have at least control of our responses to our emotions and how we look at society. We can think, judge, decide, and act, and for these things, many believe that we need to take responsibility for.

While there is no way to control the emotions, we feel in response to stimuli or outside circumstances, this theory suggests that we can control our reaction and subsequent behavior and take ownership of these things.

Only in societies where the emphasis is placed solely on the individual is this possible. The individual or self has always been an important part of Western culture, so it shouldn't be surprising that self-responsibility concepts have taken root in the West.

When people have rights, they also have responsibility. As we have gained more human rights in the West, this, too, means we hold a lot more responsibility for how we treat others, our thoughts, our reactions, and ourselves. We are expected to be responsible citizens, responsible adults, responsible employees, parents, etc.

Since we have rights to resources and obligations to those around us, we are tasked with taking charge of how well (or not well) we take responsibility for these things.

Most of us probably think we take personal responsibility, but that isn't necessarily the case. How many of us look to outside forces, factors, or actors we can blame for our life's status, our reaction to something? It is so much easier to point to something outside of oneself than to look inward to see how your emotional state may have contributed to a situation.

Like a lot of what we must do to bolster our self-esteem, taking personal responsibility isn't fun, and it can even be difficult. Many of us settle into our role as the person pulled many ways by all these outside forces beyond our control, taking away our autonomy, and thus, our responsibility for our reactions and responses.

We must break this if we want to cultivate and internalize self-responsibility.

Are You Taking Self-Responsibility?

A good way to know if you are taking self-responsibility is to ask yourself if the thoughts, emotions, and behaviors you are exhibiting help or hinder you from reaching the goal you are trying to reach? We may not be able to control our emotions in terms of how something makes us feel, but we can control how we react and take responsibility for the fact that our actions are often a result of our own emotions, not some outside factor.

We are not only responsible for the way we react to our emotions, but also, we are responsible for how we use our time and how well we care for our mental, physical, and emotional needs.

Ways to Foster Self-Responsibility

Will Joel Friedman, Ph.D., offers a helpful list of ways you can learn to take self-responsibility in your life. The first and most important way to foster this is to be present at the moment. You must be aware of your surroundings, what you are doing, and how you are feeling to take full ownership over yourself.

You will need to be honest with yourself, perhaps brutally so. None of us like accepting that something is our fault, but part of growing and developing healthy levels of confidence and feelings of self-worth make this necessary. We can never grow, change, or adapt our responses if we refuse to admit that we make mistakes or have responsibility for negative situations in our life.

Friedman notes we are responsible for what come out of our mouth, and too often, we aren't careful enough in thinking about what we say before we say it. It isn't hard to see how this cannot only get us in trouble, but is our own fault.

We also need to be consistent in our thoughts and actions. We must accept that we don't know and will never know everything about the world – or even ourselves. The goal is to learn, accept, and take responsibility – not to become a self-guru of sorts.

He also points out that life should be win/win. What he means by this is that actions should be taken into consideration more than just you. We must think about our actions in terms of their effects on others and how it affects the greater good.

Finally, he discusses the importance of being willing to change and grow. Learning about ourselves is going to bring up uncomfortable feelings and show us areas of our personality we may not be proud of or like. While some things can't be changed and just must be accepted, a lot can be changed. To take self-responsibility, you must commit to being willing to grow and change as you learn more about yourself and others.

Focusing on the external environment as the cause of our life circumstances is a mental shortcut that keeps us from seeing the key role we play. Breaking down the barrier to this understanding is key to taking self-responsibility and working to make positive changes in your life.

Chapter 6: Practicing Self-Assertiveness

Before we even begin with this chapter, we have to say a word or two about assertiveness. We all know people who are overly assertive to the point of being demanding, and nobody suggests that this is something for which we should strive. There are many who lack the ability to stand up for themselves and ask for what they need, and when referring to assertiveness here, we are this referring to.

We are talking about people who lack self-confidence and find it hard to speak up with their opinions, express their needs and emotions, or challenge someone when necessary. It's that idea of being a doormat we discussed earlier. People without healthy levels of self-assertiveness let other people dominate conversations and their life, regardless of how they feel about it inside.

What we seek to do in this chapter is to discuss the difference between being healthily assertive and aggressive, and how being too nice leads us to live inauthentic lives and can negatively affect our relationships.

The Downside of Being Nice

Being nice is good, and for some people, it should be strived for more often, but it has its limitations, and there comes the point when it turns from a positive to a negative attribute. Lest you become that metaphorical doormat, you must put a limit on your kindness for yourself and others.

But being nice isn't always the same as being honest. To avoid potential conflict or discomfort, the overly nice person may just tell others what they think they want to hear, even if it isn't true, and they don't believe it. If we are striving for authenticity in life, it should be easy to see how this is a bad thing. Authenticity means honesty, even if it is uncomfortable to do.

What seemed like a positive trait can turn into a flaw if relied upon too often. What was once a noble characteristic becomes a wall you put between the real you and the people surrounding you. Many people who are overly nice feel (and are largely right) that they are not in control over their lives and are controlled by the surrounding people.

The goal is to understand that we are doing this, and we can take back control and put ourselves in charge.

Relationships aren't and can't be as fulfilling as they could be when one party is so nice they aren't showing their true self. This can make it hard for an overly nice person to develop deep interpersonal relationships. We need not stop being nice, but we do have to stop being nice all the time, and especially telling people what we think they want to hear rather than what we think.

Our relationships will be more fulfilling when we can be honest with both others and ourselves. When we can assert ourselves at the right level, we are truly partners in our relationships. Saying what you think and ask for what you need allows your partner to give that to you. It will help your relationships become deeper and more real.

What Does it Mean to Be Self-Assertive and Why Does It Matter?

We have touched on why being self-assertive matters, but first, we should step back and look at what it means to be assertive. Then, we can dive deeper on why it is so important to cultivate self-assertiveness; beyond the brief reasons we have given.

Chances are, if you lack assertiveness, you have been told before that you need to learn to stand up for yourself and be more vocal about your wants and needs. Like everything else we discuss in this book, that is a lot easier said than done.

What even is assertiveness? It refers to your confidence and ability to communicate your thoughts, needs, feelings, and beliefs openly and honestly. It is feeling unsure about our opinions and us. We want to assert ourselves without going to the point of violating others' rights or needs, which psychologists call *aggressiveness* and which we will touch on below.

There are a lot of misconceptions about assertiveness we should look at briefly. Being assertive does not mean getting what you want all the time. That isn't the point and shouldn't be the goal. Sometimes it will mean getting what you want, but more than anything, it is ensuring that your thoughts, feelings, and needs are addressed and those of other people and not instead of.

Being assertive isn't a universal trait we have to exhibit. Sometimes, call for being assertive and others where it isn't necessary. You are making a mistake if you assume that to self-assert, you must do so in every interpersonal interaction. Doing so will probably lead to conflict and unnecessary stress.

Failure to assert oneself can have a huge effect on self-esteem. It can make you feel as if your thoughts, feelings, and needs don't matter, and over time, you stop putting any emphasis on your own personal needs. People who cannot assert themselves often live lives directed and controlled (whether knowingly or not) by those around them.

People unable to express their thoughts or needs often keep them to themselves, even in situations it would benefit them to express their needs. This can lead to increased anxiousness, depression, and even resentment towards the people we have relinquished control to. Seeing as how it was us that relinquished control, it isn't fair to blame others for this situation.

People with generalized or social anxiety often report great difficulty asserting themselves in their daily lives. We fear ridicule and judgment, which can cause us to retract from society and develop unhealthy relationships with the people we interact with.

Assertiveness, or a lack thereof, is a learned skill. It is something we develop throughout our life experiences. Take a baby, for example. They cry when they want or need something and will learn to adapt their behavior to get most easily what they want or need. Adults do this, as well.

A baby (or a child or an adult) that doesn't get a positive response when they try to ask for what they need may develop a tendency to fail to assert to get what they need. If you come from a family where one member dominates the rest or unhealthy dialogue and communication is the norm, you may have self-assertiveness issues.

Some peer groups may even make you feel bad or selfish for having your own wants and needs, and we learn this over time, which leads us to shut off this part of ourselves. Due to this, we can turn into that figurative doormat easily.

A lot of things keep us from asserting ourselves when we need to. Many of us have a loud inner critic that tells us we lack, that we don't have the right skill or talent, and that we will embarrass ourselves if we express our opinions aloud. For many of us, this is enough to stifle us to the point we can't assert ourselves.

Some of us just don't have the skills or practice necessary to be self-assertive. The key is to learn and develop these skills so you can gain enough confidence to assert yourself in appropriate situations.

Being stressed or dealing with high anxiety can often shut us down, figuratively. It can make asserting ourselves feel like an impossible or pointless task. The problem is that failure to be assertive can also create higher levels of anxiety or stress. It can become a vicious cycle.

We also have cultural influences that affect how assertive we feel we can be. In many societies, women are supposed to be quiet and docile, and for them to express themselves assertively would be a faux pas. It can be hard to figure out how to handle assertiveness when the underlying factor keeping one from asserting themselves is cultural. Unfortunately, how to deal with this is beyond the scope of this book.

In Western society, assertiveness and being self-assured is not only valued but also encouraged, at least on the surface.

Assertiveness vs. Aggression

As we noted in the chapter opening, assertiveness differs from being aggressive. Aggressive people dominate others around them and act out when that domination is challenged. Assertive people simply make sure their needs are met, and their feelings are expressed.

Aggressive people rarely have much regard for the surrounding people. They want what they want and will do what they need to get it, even at the expense of someone else. If they don't get their way, they are likely to act out in an unhinged manner. The assertive person has a lot of regard for the people around them and takes both themselves and others into consideration before speaking or acting.

There is a tendency for an overly aggressive person to become a bully. Here is another key difference between someone who is aggressive and assertive. The aggressive person is a bully, whereas the assertive person is seeking not to be bullied.

Becoming More Self-Assertive

Of all the things we ask people to do to cultivate self-esteem, understanding and accepting yourself and being more self-assertive tend to the most difficult steps. People who are not used to expressing or speaking up for themselves find it doesn't come naturally and must be forced for a while, if not forever.

You must have confidence to be assertive about your feelings and your needs. Working on developing your self-confidence, which we explore in-depth in the next chapter, is part of developing the ability to be self-assertive when necessary.

Just a quick example is confidence in your beliefs. Until you have confidence that you understand your views and beliefs and have the data and evidence back it, you will have a hard time convincing someone else that you are right. If you aren't even sure about what you are saying, why should someone believe it?

We can't let others decide how we feel about something or shape our opinions; otherwise, they aren't our own. This requires us to take control of our own feelings or emotions, which also means we must value ourselves enough not to care if someone disagrees with us on something we feel strongly about.

Being self-assertive also requires us to value other people more than an overly nice person does. This might sound harsh, but we do have to accept that when we tell others what they want to hear, we are lying to them, which indicates a lack of value we place on them, even if we don't mean to.

If you value someone, you will want to tell him or her the whole truth, even if it hurts or makes you uncomfortable. You must let someone know who you are, and if you hide your opinions behind constant agreement or platitudes, then they don't know you. When someone you care about hurts you, you should want to tell them about it so they can grow and hopefully not do whatever it is again. If you don't tell them, you deny them the opportunity to grow and become better to you.

A solid and healthy relationship requires honest and active participation from both parties.

Becoming more self-assertive means developing courage—courage in your convictions and in your worth. This is, of course, far easier said than done, but it clearly takes personal courage to tell the truth and ask for what we want or need. Conversations and relationships require us to be vulnerable. While this is uncomfortable, it is a vital part of happy, deep relationships. It takes guts and courage to go into an emotionally charged situation, willing to bare your soul, but the results will be good even if it isn't readily apparent at first.

Many people don't even know where to begin when it comes to being more self-assertive. One way to become more assertive and more effective in communication is to take possession of emotions. Say someone insults you. Rather than saying something like "that was mean," take ownership and try something like, "I was hurt when you said that."

It also helps to focus on the behavior rather than the person expressing the behavior. Usually it isn't the person themselves that makes you upset, but rather, their *actions*. So, focus on the action rather than making it personal. They are less likely to respond defensively if you address the behavior so it makes it about the action and doesn't treat it as a personal failing or character flaw.

We also need to discuss the importance of letting the other person have time to understand. After you have asserted yourself, you must allow the person time to change or respond. You can't expect them to act immediately, and if you do, you are being unfair and are not likely to get a positive result.

You must be present and observant in your life and relationships so you can see where you are failing and where you are allowing others to control your life. You must know yourself well enough to know what you want and need before you can ask for it. Perhaps most important, believe that you have a right to an opinion and a say in what happens in your life and your place in the world. None of this is easy, but we wouldn't have so many people dealing with self-esteem issues if it were.

Being assertive doesn't mean always getting your way. Rather, it is a balance between what you need and what others need, as opposed to solely being about what others need. It isn't selfish to consider yourself in a situation that directly affects you. The important part is that both your and others' needs are addressed and considered equally. You aren't trying to "win" or have your opinion dominate the conversation; you just want to be a part of the conversation and have your needs or concerns addressed. It's about being part of the conversation, not taking it over. Again, this is a key difference between being assertive and aggressive.

Chapter 7: Self-Esteem and Pop Culture

Celebrity and pop culture are part of society, whether we like it or not. Though it is easy to see where too much focus on celebrity culture could lead to self-esteem issues, using social media and its connection with self-esteem issues is just getting quality research. With celebrity, it's hard to compete with the looks, money, and material success celebrities have, and if we use this as our measuring stick for our own success, chances are our self-esteem will suffer.

The biggest problem with both celebrity and social media is not that they exist, per se; it is more that too many of us use them as a comparison for our own success, worth, and value to the world. Celebrity culture and social media are often far from reality, which makes the comparison inherently unfair.

Whether we should or not, we make comparisons between others and ourselves. The biggest issue is whom we use as our comparison group. Before the advent of social media, we were more limited to basic celebrity culture and our peer group - our friends, family, coworkers, neighbors, etc. Comparisons between more everyday people and ourselves tend to give us a better indication of our own level of success as it relates to society. We do not get this when our biggest social comparison group is social media-related.

Social media and pop culture dominate our lives to a large extent. How many of us go for more than a few hours without checking social media? We even live in a time where actual important world news may be broken via social media, so eliminating it from our lives isn't necessarily an option, but we can alter how we look at social media and the way we use it.

There is nothing wrong with simply enjoying the glitz and glamor of celebrity culture or even social media personalities we enjoy following. Except, it is helpful to remember that what we see in these spaces is carefully cultivated and isn't unfiltered reality like we might at first think. There are healthy ways to enjoy celebrity culture and social media, but too often, we let it have a negative impact on what we think about ourselves and the value or interest of our own lives. Behold, this is where the problem lies.

We should point out that not all celebrity culture and social media are bad. Like anything, these things can be either good or bad, depending on how we use them and the value we place on it. There are also campaigns for body positivity and celebrities who invite us into their lives to see it isn't as glamorous as it might first appear and that they deal with real everyday problems just like everyone else.

One of the biggest problems is so many of us don't see how much of what we see on social media is an illusion.

Social Media Reality vs. Actual Reality

Most of us spend at least part of our day browsing social media. We are exposed to tons of content, news, some from people like us, and some from people who seem to live charmed and glamorous lives. Some content can be uplifting and inspire us to take chances or to change our lives, but a lot of the content seems to make us feel worse about ourselves.

Look at all these people who are prettier than you, more successful than you, or live more interesting lives. What do they have, and what is wrong with you that you *don't*? Too many of us go through this when we become mired in social media, and it makes it hard for us to be satisfied with ourselves and where we are in life. There will always be someone more successful or exciting than us, and it is detrimental to our mental health to feel bad we can't keep up.

Just think about it. Spending your day looking into the lives of people who seem smarter, happier, more successful, richer, more attractive, or more talented than you can be inspirational only for so long before it makes you feel as though you are lacking. Why aren't you as attractive, as smart or as interesting as social media personalities you like to follow? What do you lack?

But you lack nothing. It helps to remember just how contrived social media and celebrity culture is. Almost none of the content we see from these people is organic. They had makeup artists and wardrobe help them get their look just right. They have professional photographers that help them stage their photos just right. Plus, that amazing "candid" shot you just liked might have been the 20th take of the picture attempt.

The point is that *this isn't reality*. It is staged and framed to make the surroundings look perfect and luxurious than they are. We all want to put ourselves in the best possible light, and celebrities are no different; they just have more money and tools to make this happen than the rest of us.

Staged photos, stylists, carefully framed shots, and extensive filters and editing go into most of what we see online. The point of harping on this is to show this is not reality; it is an illusion of what someone wants to represent his or her reality to be. Sadly, if you believe that everything you see online is real and organic then you are sorely mistaken.

Most people don't show the mundane or bleaker parts of life, especially celebrities and social media influencers that are trying to maintain a persona. There is a fine line between finding this content motivating and this content distressing because it makes us feel less than. A lot of time, being mired in this content will make us feel bad about ourselves because we are not as talented, attractive, or successful as the people we look up to and follow.

Celebrities and influencers seem perpetually happy, busy, and living the best life, which can make someone scrolling through social media in their pajamas while eating popcorn feel bad about himself or herself. We feel like failures in the face of these seemingly perfect people who are always happy and always on the go, doing something far more exciting than what we do.

We don't see them dealing with dog poop or dirty laundry, and although celebrities largely have people who will do these things for them, it isn't like every part of their life is picture-perfect, or that they get out of bed with flawless makeup and clothing. They are presenting an image, and that image leaves a lot out while adding a lot of fake in. To a far lesser extent, many of us also do this when we post online, so we should just expect this from anyone on social media or in celebrity culture. They are trying to sell a product, even if that product is the envy of their lifestyle.

In American society, particularly, celebrity culture has been elevated to an high level. People with few skills or redeeming qualities can become overnight celebrities thanks to reality television and social media. We are shown these people live charmed lives far more interesting and action-packed than our own, and we look at our own lives as if they should be more like television.

And we also have a tendency to fetishize wealth and look at people with more money than we could ever dream of as if they are the model we should aspire to and measure our own success against - no matter how unrealistic or unattainable this might prove to be. Capitalism has allowed for the creation of many success stories, but there are also stories of failure or potential not met that we don't hear about because they don't make good news stories.

But it's motivating to know that other people fail and experience doubt and basic life frustrations just like you. When all we see is a happy, idealized version of someone's life, it can give us the false sense that something about them makes them immune from negative feelings and that frustrations aren't something they have to deal with because they are more or "better."

So much of the value we place on ourselves is based on how we feel we stack up against other people. Constantly comparing ourselves to celebrities and social media influencers is bound to make us feel like we are lesser or lacking. When we use these people as our guide for our own success, happiness, and value, social media and consumption of celebrity culture become negative factors for our self-esteem. There will always be some hot new star that is young, beautiful and seems to have it all. It isn't easy to see, but it is important to know that much of this is simply a presentation; it *isn't reality*.

It is natural to compare oneself to others. In the past, we might have marginally looked at celebrities and thought about what charmed lives they lived, but we seemed to understand this was unattainable and not something most of us can strive for. Much of our self-comparison was with other people in our community including our friends, family, and neighbors. Most of which are on roughly the same material level as us, and thus, more realistic comparisons of our own relative success in the material world.

Fast forward to today, and we are no longer comparing ourselves with our neighbors or that guy in class you are always trying to edge out for best grade. Rather, we are comparing ourselves to celebrities, wealthy personalities, and social media influencers with a ton of money, equipment, and means to make their lives look far more exciting than we could ever hope for.

This is called the upward comparison, and when done modestly, it can be motivating for us to take risks and try more. But when that is the only comparison, it is easy to see how we can quickly feel bad about ourselves. We can't stack up against wealthy celebrities with a team of people who help keep them looking as good as humanly possible whenever they are in public.

It is a huge mistake to consider what we see on social media to be real life and use it to measure the value of our own lives. As we already noted, most of what you see on social media and especially in celebrity magazines is highly filtered, posed, and, well, *contrived.* It isn't reality; it is a *well-crafted illusion.*

Self-presentation is a huge part of social media, and we all try to make ourselves look good most of the time. For example, even regular folks will move a pile of dirty laundry out of a picture, so it looks like their surroundings are perfect and far less cluttered than they are. It's helpful to understand how even we present a false picture of ourselves when we use social media since we, too, try to frame ourselves and our pictures in the best light.

If you are experiencing confidence issues, it's helpful to look closely at your social media usage. Is social media the biggest benchmark you use for comparison? What types of people do you follow? If you spend much of your social time using social media and follow very few "regular people," chances are your experience isn't always positive. It can be fun and even inspiring to look at the lives of those with a lot more than you, but this can't be the only group you have to compare yourself. You also must remember just how much of what you see is manufactured.

Negative Effects of Social Media

Social media not only takes up a lot of our time, but there is also a lot of new research that shows those of us who use social media a lot may be more likely to have mental health issues than those who are only casual users. Chou and Edge performed a study in 2012 that showed that frequent Facebook users tend to think others are happier and more successful than themselves.

But when we compare ourselves to what we see on social media, it is like comparing our actual real life, with all its mess, to a carefully crafted, idealized presentation. Basically, it is an unfair and unrealistic comparison, but many of us fall into this trap. Unfortunately, it can have very negative impacts on how we view our value to the world and ourselves in general.

Even when interacting with people closer to being peers in terms of material success and the like, we often use arbitrary and useless measures that mean nothing to compare ourselves with them. For example, how many followers does someone have compared to you? How many likes do their pictures get versus yours? We all do this, but it is silly when you think about it. There are inorganic ways of getting likes and follows, and it doesn't matter. Numbers do not affect value or worth. We shouldn't base our usefulness or value on statistics like this, but we do, all too often.

It seems that the more immersed we are in celebrity and social media culture, the more likely it is to have a negative impact on our self-esteem and overall mental health. Studies by Feinstein and others in 2013 showed that people who use social media excessively report higher depression rates and a lower sense of wellbeing.

Chronic social media users are also likely to report lower levels of self-esteem than casual users, indicating a correlation between the amount of time we spend in the virtual space and our sense of wellbeing. This is likely because, in the virtual space, we are more likely to engage in upward social comparison with people with things we can never hope to have. Chronic users are constantly exposed to people who seem "better" than they are, and this can naturally have negative effects on how they feel about themselves.

Some people are better at moderating their social media usage than others and can easily limit themselves with things like screen time monitors. Other people can't do this, and to get out of that trap, we might have to spend time away from social media to ensure that we don't let it take over our lives and become negative to our overall wellbeing and self-esteem.

Positive Elements of Social Media

When used casually and with the right mindset, social media is a fun distraction and can even motivate at times. It can be a great way to blow off steam or interact with people who share the same interests. The problem isn't social media itself, so much as using this virtual space as our primary means for self-comparison with others. We discussed earlier that it is far less "real" than we might originally think.

As much as we have focused on negative aspects of social media, there are also motivating and uplifting elements of it and celebrity culture. We have recently seen a lot more body positive content, including the rise of plus-size models that give us something beyond the stick-thin Barbie to aspire to. Body positivity aims to help regular people feel better about their imperfect selves and give people better, more realistic role models.

This is a good thing for many reasons. Foremost, most of us can't aspire to look like a runway model. Those people must work exceptionally hard for their bodies, and it can be a full-time job to look the way they do. People come in all shapes and sizes, and beauty isn't one-size-fits-all. We can strive to become healthier versions of ourselves, but we also must accept what our body looks like to some extent. Especially for younger generations, not having any role models that look like normal people can have detrimental effects, so any furthering of body positivity is good for current and future generations.

More brands are coming out with plus size clothing and using models of all shapes and sizes in their advertising, which is a good thing. This gives us more than one "shape" of the body that is the one we should strive for. It helps us feel like we are okay as we are, even if we aren't tall and thin like the Victoria Secret models. The rise in more plus size clothing options provides more inclusivity, and even higher-end brands such as Rihanna's Savage X Fenty now offer plus sizes, which is not something we would have seen even just a few years ago.

For a long time, bigger people were limited in the clothes available to them. They were frumpy and not at all what was in fashion, which went further to making plus-sized people feel like something was wrong with them. Seeing more brands offer cutting edge plus-size trends, and more luxury brands also expanding their offerings goes a long way towards both self-acceptance and societal acceptance of a multitude of beauty standards.

Some celebrities are using social media to help break the idea of a "perfect star" with a charmed life and no problems. They are letting people into the darker and messier parts of their lives by sharing their battles with mental illness or even difficult pregnancies. This might not seem like much, but with all the sanitized and artificial content we typically consume, hearing celebrities who seem so much "more" than us talking about problems we deal with can help bring them down from the pedestal we placed them on and make them seem more like regular people with real-life problems.

In recent years, social media has raised concerns about mental health, body image, and more. Men's mental health and body positivity are finally starting to get notice and attention, which is great. While women face a lot of beauty and other standards, men to face these. They are told they shouldn't be emotional and that it is a character flaw if they struggle with mental issues. We are seeing this paradigm shift, which is wonderful, since we all need to feel comfortable and okay with asking for help when we need it. Needing help is part of being human. It is starting to be "okay" for a man to seek mental health care, but there is still a stigma largely attached to it.

Many men "aren't okay" and would benefit from mental health services but have been made to feel as if they are showing weakness or are lesser men if they ask for help. So many tragedies and lives of quiet depression could be avoided if people felt as if it were okay to ask for help when they needed it. These campaigns aimed at men are trying to normalize the idea that sometimes men need help too, and there is nothing to be ashamed of. This is a sadly deeply engrained idea likely to take generations to work out.

While different, men, too, deal with issues of body image. Just think about the "quintessential man"; he is young and fit with a full head of hair. You get the idea. Like with the stereotypical "perfect woman," very few men fit these standards, and it affects self-esteem and feelings of self-worth. Body positivity for men, women, non-binary people is a good thing for our mental health all around, and we hope this trend continues.

We have also seen more age-positive content. Social media and celebrity culture focus on youth, and as we age, it can seem like we become less and less important to society. Older celebrities and even social media personalities are opening up about aging and their feelings surrounding it and the unique challenges they face as stars when they age. This can help us feel empowered by our age, rather than ashamed, which is important in our youth-driven celebrity culture.

Basically, celebrities have been letting us into their lives behind all the illusion to see what they are like. They get pimples, experience setbacks, and have issues. Because we look up to them so much, there can be something empowering about discovering that your favorite celebrity has also dealt with doubt and sought help in the process. If even they need those kinds of things, how can we fault ourselves as "mere mortals" for needing it as well?

Finally, untouched photos and those free of filters have become a "thing" among celebrities and social media influencers. These are actually real pictures, not ones staged and filtered to perfection. Celebrities are sharing pictures of themselves without makeup, with bedhead, and in other real-life situations we can relate to because, well, they are real. This helps break the stereotype that people who live "better" than we don't suffer from basic irritations of life and perhaps, at times, don't look perfect.

We have a lot of hope these trends will continue, and transparency becomes more the norm. We can tell you until we are blue in the face that celebrities and social media personalities are just humans with their own issues and faults, but if you never see it but constantly see your own, it's hard to believe this. As they allow us into their real lives, showing us the good and the bad, social media usage becomes a little less problematic as it jives more with reality than an idealized version of it.

It's hard to find that balance between healthy social media usage and consumption of celebrity culture and using it so much and in such a way it has a detrimental impact on our life and our feelings. When used casually, it can be a fun distraction or allow us to interact with people who share our interests. Occasionally looking at celebrity content can even have a motivating factor for some of us.

The big thing is keeping everything in perspective. Often, what is on social media is engineered and, well, not actual reality. Celebrities don't roll out of bed looking perfect and don't leave the gym looking flawless without effort. A lot of behind-the-scenes work goes into what seems like candid photos or content we often forget about. It is an illusion of reality, not actual reality.

It is also important to limit the amount of upward comparison we do when thinking about how we stack up against others. Looking up to highly successful people isn't a bad thing but when this is the only social group we use for comparison, it can have a negative impact on our lives. We must be realistic with our social comparisons. We will get a much better idea of what our lives look like to others when we compare ourselves with the person down the street than the latest big Hollywood celeb. Better still would be to stop comparing ourselves to others, which we will look at in the next chapter.

Chapter 8: Start Building Your Confidence

In a variety of ways, we have shown how important it is to have self-confidence, but for those lacking confidence, gaining it doesn't come naturally or easily. It is easy to tell people they need more confidence; however, this doesn't help them or tell them anything they don't already know. Most people lacking in self-confidence are perfectly aware of this lacking; they just aren't sure how to fix it.

We can do a lot of things that will help us begin to look at ourselves with more kindness and gain a sense of confidence that allows us to take more control over our lives, wants, and needs. Though it must first be stated: no one thing works for everyone, and this requires effort. For people telling themselves for years they aren't worthy and don't matter, it takes a lot more than a positive mantra to make them believe and internalize this.

The ability to trust our own judgment and abilities is important in many areas of life. Having confidence allows us to ask for what we need and results in better careers and more meaningful interpersonal relationships. Self-confidence is important because it enables us to have the courage to take risks, express our emotions, or ask for what we want or need in life. Sadly, for people with low self-esteem, confidence is severely lacking or even nonexistent, and changing this doesn't happen overnight.

It is important for both our physical and mental wellbeing to have a healthy level of self-confidence. Confidence can make you more willing to try new things and consider taking on challenges that might prove very meaningful or fruitful for your life. It also helps you become a better communicator, as you are more self-assured when it comes to the worth of your wants, needs, feelings, and ideas. Lacking self-confidence makes so many things a struggle that can, in turn, reinforce negative self-feelings, that turn into an ugly, self-perpetuating cycle of negativity.

How to Improve Your Confidence

One of the first things we need to do to boost our confidence concerns social comparisons. As discussed in the chapter on social media and celebrity culture, too much upward social comparison can cause negative impacts on our self-outlook because we are giving ourselves an unreasonable comparison. We can take this further, though, because we really shouldn't be comparing ourselves to others as it is.

We are not only all different, but we are also at different stages in life, and we have different goals and abilities. This can make comparing one person to another like comparing apples to oranges - we are not comparing the same things, and thus the comparison isn't helpful. It might seem like it's motivating to try to compete with others and use them as our standard for comparison; it also reduces our confidence and may even make us less sure of our own skill and ability.

Though this seems obvious, we are not other people. They haven't had the same life experience. They don't have the same inner mentality. They do not have the skills or challenges we have. We have had a unique experience and are unique creatures that really shouldn't be compared with other unique creatures with different circumstances and situations than our own.

We should be our comparisons, not anyone else. There is a fine line between envy and the way we ultimately feel about ourselves, and when we remove those upward comparisons and use ourselves as our measure of how far we've come in life, we get a much more accurate picture. Life isn't a competition anyway. When looking at ourselves, we should be thinking about how far we have come in our life's journey, the obstacles we have overcome, the challenges we have met, and how we can leverage our skills and abilities to better improve our lives.

Another important part of developing self-confidence and a positive outlook requires self-care. We must take care of ourselves physically, mentally, and spiritually if we want to live our best lives. We have stated this multiple times and will discuss it again, but if you aren't taking care of yourself, it is hard to feel good about anything. You will not feel great physically, and you probably won't like what you see when you look in the mirror if you ignore your own health and wellbeing.

We must address our personal needs if we want to be happy, healthy, and successful people. Our bodies need proper sleep, food, hydration, activity, and personal time. Things like a physical activity not only help us look and feel better physically, but it can also help improve our mood and overall mental wellbeing, which can make it easier to gain confidence about oneself.

Again, we must state something that should be obvious but may not be—practicing self-care is not selfish; it is reasonable and responsible.

Having compassion for ourselves will also help us become more accepting of ourselves and will help us our journey to boost our self-confidence. We must give ourselves a break. We aren't perfect. Nobody is perfect. There will never be a perfect human. And that's okay! Everybody experiences failure, shame, embarrassment, and disappointment. It is okay to feel these emotions, but we should try to feel them with tenderness, the way we would look at the misfortune of someone we love.

We need to work towards speaking more kindly to ourselves, especially when we are down. Kindness is more motivating for most of us than constant negative self-talk. For many, these constant feelings of lacking act as a barrier, stopping them from moving forward with any aspect of their life and thus contributing to more negative feelings about themselves.

Everyone experiences failure. Everyone. Having a setback is not an indictment of your value or worth to society; it is a human experience we all must face. Again, try to give yourself a break and look at yourself the way you would look at your closest friend who just suffered a setback. Being able to treat ourselves with compassion and care will help us understand that we deserve to feel our feelings but also, that we are not "the worst" because we made a mistake.

Self-doubt is something that even the most successful person deals with, but the big difference is that they address the doubt and then move on. Doubt is a normal part of the human experience and can be a good thing since it makes us look more closely at our decisions and get advice or feedback from others that can help us make better choices. It is okay to have doubt - in fact, it would be an issue if we never had any - but the problem arises when we let this doubt keep us from trying or acting.

Acting, even if you fail, can often improve confidence because you TRIED. Trying is a huge deal. It takes a ton of courage, and even in failure, there is a lot to learn if we are willing. Prepare, practice, but don't let the fear of failure stop you from trying. You'll never be 100% confident about most things, and life will always have some doubt. But we must learn how to harness and control this doubt so it can guide our choices but not let it control us and keep us from even attempting something.

You will also need to challenge yourself (not that what we have discussed isn't challenging, of course). We mean that when you engage in negative self-talk, you need to challenge that self-talk. Address that negative inner critic and engage it. Tell the voice is wrong and just trying to hold you back. It is irrational, and you will not keep listening to it.

Our negative thoughts are often wrong, and if we probe them a little, that will become plain to see. Looking at our inner critic more closely will let us better determine when it has legitimate criticism and when it is irrational.

Actionable Steps Towards Self-Confidence

A lot of what we have talked about so far is rather abstract, but it is vitally important for developing healthy levels of self-confidence. One great way to start on this journey to improved self-confidence is to list all the achievements and strengths you have, no matter how small. Seriously, list everything, even if you are listing something as seemingly inconsequential as being a good whistler. This list should show you that even where you are right now, you have a lot of strengths.

Refer back to this list often so you never forget where you've come from and what you have accomplished. Add to this list as you go. As your confidence grows, so too will the strengths we allow ourselves to see.

Though it won't come naturally at first, try to think positively about yourself. Force yourself if necessary. You don't even have to focus on something major; it can be a small thing. Say you made a killer grilled cheese sandwich. Take a minute to pat yourself on the back for what a good job you did. Little things like this will allow you to see that you do positive things and have positive qualities readily apparent if we let ourselves see them.

You will want to set realistic challenges for yourself for raising your self-confidence. This can be as simple as making yourself say positive daily mantras or taking a few minutes to journal about the positive aspects of your day. The more you surround yourself with positivity, the more it will positively affect your overall mood and your wellbeing. Setting tiny goals, such as making sure you get proper hydration for a week, then achieving said goal, can go a long way in helping to improve self-confidence. When you see yourself reaching these goals, it is hard to feel bad about yourself.

Again, you will want to make sure you are engaging in self-care since when we look and feel good, it will often affect your mental outlook.

Do you have a list of things you've always wanted to do? Dust off that list and reconsider it. What on the list is realistic or attainable? Make a new list with these realistic goals, add any you can think of, and make a real plan as to how to achieve these goals.

It can also be helpful to evaluate your social circle and involve them in your efforts to improve your self-confidence. You need a social network of supportive people who see the good in you, not people who bring you down or make you feel like everything is a competition. Consciously practice kindness with yourself and others, even if it doesn't feel natural. Over time, it will become part of who you are, and you can do this without giving it much thought.

Chapter 9: How to Live with Purpose

For most people, meaning and purpose are what they are looking for in life, but many of us have no idea how to do this. Feeling like we are just floating through life on autopilot is not a good feeling, and it isn't surprising that since so many of us do this because we have issues with self-esteem and feelings of self-worth. Nobody likes to feel as if they have no control in their life, and it's hard to find a purpose in a life not controlled by you.

We have discussed numerous times how you can take back control of your life, feelings, and opinions, so we won't go into detail about it here. We all want our lives to be fulfilling and to give us a sense that we are involved with something bigger than ourselves. This seems to be a common human goal across the ages and across cultures. So why is it so difficult?

Life is busy; we work, we have obligations, and perhaps we have children too. This can make us feel like we are pulled in so many directions while we never even stop to think about the purpose or meaning of our life, but we also live with the vague sense of being unfulfilled.

If we are brave enough to do what is needed to take control of our lives, we have a lot of choice in how we live them. Too many of us live our lives based on what we think society wants from us, which, in effect, takes control of our own existence away from us and puts it into the hands of this vague concept of "societal norms." Being unhappy and unsatisfied with our lives makes us feel bad, out of control, and can become a vicious cycle of self-doubt and self-hatred.

While it isn't easy and will take time, you can take that control over your life back and live with meaning and purpose. It will take time. It involves figuring out what you value, believe, and what is important in life. How can these values be used to help further the greater good? No matter what you think is important, whether it be adult literacy or concern about stray animals and their well-being, there are ways you can make this value a driving force in your life.

What is Involved in a Meaningful Life?

The world was here before us and will continue on after us, and this can make us feel inconsequential and meaningless, but when we find ways to connect ourselves to causes or ideas that are bigger than ourselves and will continue on after we are gone, we can start to feel like we are part of something with far greater meaning and value than one human life.

This "bigger purpose" is something that we may spend much, if not all, our lives searching for. We need something that will enrich us mentally and spiritually, that we also feel to value for the future and is addressing an issue or cause that will affect lives far beyond just our own.

We live beyond ourselves when we participate in movements that affect not just our lives but those of generations to come. This is why so many people who feel as if they live purposeful and meaningful lives are part of causes bigger than themselves and that they feel will have a positive impact on society.

Whether we like animals, are concerned about social justice, or are passionate about STEM fields being more prominent in public schools, we all have an interest in something with an effect on more than just us and can contribute to the greater good. Getting involved with movements or activities like this will help us feel like we are part of the greater society, doing things that positively contribute to our future.

Many people feel as if they find their "calling" when they get involved in a movement or organization that tackles an important issue. It can also be rewarding to help others struggling to find their calling. Not only will this make you feel good about yourself; it can help other people.

When you are involved with something you are passionate about, it doesn't feel like work, and it feels like you have found a home. This sense of purpose and meaning has a value that cannot be quantified.

We can also help ourselves live a life with meaning and purpose by engaging in life with love and self-confidence. This, of course, is a lot easier said than done. Having something in your life, like a cause that makes you feel engaged with something larger than yourself, can help you find greater levels of self-esteem, as you feel engrossed with life and part of the group so it is hard to find anywhere else. When we do something for the greater good, it becomes much harder to tell ourselves that we are lacking or unworthy of love and respect.

Benefits of a Purposeful Life

It might seem like living a life of meaning and purpose is self-evident, good, and that is correct, but the benefits of living a meaningful life go beyond just making it easier to convince us we have value and are deserving of a good life.

When we feel like we are living meaningful lives, the normal pitfalls of everyday life can become easier to bear. Those who are involved in causes or organizations that give them a sense of purpose often report they have an easier time dealing with and moving on from disappointment and failure. It becomes easier to let go of ill will towards others and yourself and to move on from negative elements of your past.

When our lives have meaning, we learn how to better embrace life and live with gratitude and compassion. We spend our time engaged in good and beneficial behavior. When life feels like it has value and meaning, we can expand our mental horizons and gain empathy, which helps us accept ourselves and makes us more accepting of others. We learn to better understand others' actions and feelings, which is beneficial for all involved because it makes us better communicators and friends.

We all have a system of values and beliefs, even if we have spent little time thinking about them. This is the time to think about what you feel and believe; what you think brings value to your life. When you know what you value and think, you can live more in accordance with those values.

Living a purposeful life also requires you to have realistic goals and set realistic priorities. We should spend as much time as we possibly can on activities that further our value and provide good to the world at large, but it is important not to overdo it. We must have balance in our lives. Just like we need a good work/life balance, we also need balance in our efforts to make the world a better place. We aren't much use to the world if we are exhausted and malnourished.

Living a life of meaning requires us to be present at the moment and to pay attention to what is going on around us. This can also help us reduce distraction and to pay more attention to our internal needs.

Man's search for meaning and purpose is a quest as old as mankind itself, and it is often a lifelong process. Viktor Frankl, an influential Austrian psychologist, said that finding meaning in our existence is one of our life's defining forces, even if we aren't actively aware of this. We can give meaning and purpose to our lives, depending on what matters to us, our abilities, and where our values lie.

On a personal level, knowing and living by your values is not just a generally meaningful life, but a life with personal purpose. On a bigger-picture level, we look to be part of something that goes beyond our short time on this earth. For most of us, the big picture purpose will involve giving. That might mean giving time, love, thought, or even money.

Those who have found purpose are happier than those who feel like their life lacks meaning. They also have confidence and are surer of themselves. Since we all seek meaning and purpose, as Frankl noted, this is a very human journey that might be the ultimate expression of what it means to be a human.

Some people find their meaning and calling early in life, but many of us aren't that lucky. We can know that what we are doing is giving us meaning and purpose when work doesn't feel like work. Instead, it feels like a hobby or another form of personal enrichment. Your actions start to become an extension of your values, and you will often lose yourself in the work because it is some immersive to your very being.

Sometimes, especially if we are struggling to find a meaning or purpose, we need to pull back from our daily life. Breaking out of routine drudgery is also necessary. We have to figure out who we are, where our values lie, and what is truly important for us if we want to find ways to live a life filled with meaning and purpose.

Chapter 10: Meditation as a Mindful Practice

Meditation has long been a daily part of life for billions of people, especially for those from Eastern cultures. It has continued to gain popularity in recent decades and is now even commonly practiced by many people throughout the West. There is a good reason for this, as this ancient practice is invaluable to countless people across space and time.

Meditation is one of the most important of the mindfulness practices. Mindfulness simply refers to the ability to be mindful of and live in the moment. It is taking the time to observe your surroundings, inner feelings and live life more deliberately and with greater gratitude and purpose. Because of what is involved in the practice, meditation helps get you in the here and now and provides the ability to help you find mental clarity, reduce stress, and find greater value and purpose in life.

It is helpful to calm your mind and allow yourself to get rid of the inconsequential thoughts that inundate us daily. We must remove ourselves from the hustle and bustle and steal moments for us to just be and to just experience the present as a means to manage the stresses of the future better.

Before we get into how to meditate, we need to make a huge forewarning: meditation is HARD. It isn't easy. It is difficult. Any other way of something not coming naturally, you need to illustrate the point. Being in the moment with our minds still and calm is almost the antithesis of modern society, and being creatures of modern society, it is hard to remove ourselves from the mindset we always need to go, go, go.

Meditation takes practice, and for many people, it is years before, if they ever, learn to master the practice. If you find meditation difficult, good, that means you are in good company. Most people do, which is why it takes years to master. The effort is worth it as we get value from the mere practice of meditation, even if it isn't as successful as we would like it to be.

The Science of Meditation

Many people swear by meditation, a practice used by millions for centuries, but is there any science to back up the claims of its benefits? It turns out there actually is. We should note this has been studied for decades, and there is promising current research that is ongoing, but there are difficulties with this type of research due to the nature of what we are seeking to understand. We will discuss this more below.

There have been several studies into the value and efficacy of many mindfulness practices, but meditation is one of the most important.

One thing science has shown us is that the practice of meditation helps us with our attention. If we have short attention spans, it can help us hold our focus for longer. It helps us stay present, so we are open and aware of new information and stimuli that we might often ignore out of habit.

Evidence shows that the long-term practice of meditation can reduce overall stress levels. This isn't to say that people who meditate never experience stress, but rather that they experience it at lower rates and appear to be much better suited in dealing with stress in a healthy manner. It appears that the process of meditation allows us to slow down and process things in a healthier manner, to have a clearer mind, which can make us more adaptable to changes.

Research from prominent educational institutions has also shown that meditation can help reduce the effects of certain health conditions from irritable bowel syndrome to fibromyalgia, but there should be some caution in taking too much from these studies just yet. There have been complaints about the methodology used or the small sample sizes employed in these studies, which could affect the ability to generalize these results to the population.

More rigorous and randomized controlled studies are now being used to make more sense of this data and determine how much value we can place on the results. There are issues that will make any research on this subject difficult, and part of it is the subjective nature of the phenomena we wish to study.

One of the biggest problems facing researchers is common – small sample sizes. The larger a sample population you can use in your study, the more likely it will generally apply to society. Many of the studies conducted have fewer than 100 participants, and these participants' demographics may not represent society as a whole. Commonly, this can limit what can be gleaned from these studies.

Another difficulty is the ambiguity in the definition of terms like mindfulness and the many types of meditation practiced. Who is to say that one type of meditation isn't superior to others? When we say participants in a study practiced meditation, what kind of mediation? In what setting did they practice and for how long? As you can see, the variety of types of practice, and the slippery nature of a definition of mindfulness, has made this a pretty difficult area of study.

Recent research from Harvard also shows there may be positive benefits for depressed individuals who practice meditation. This is not a "miracle cure." Studies have shown there is a moderate positive effect for people who practice meditation, but it will not take the place of medication or therapy. Rather, it is just one more tool in our therapeutic arsenal for dealing with stress and depression.

Studies and reviews of studies show evidence that the practice of mediation may have tangible effects on our brain and its functioning. There are current studies underway by the NCCIH into the effects of meditation on chronic pain, stress reduction in people with a range of specific conditions, and how it can affect ailments like headaches or reduce blood pressure.

This exciting research could give much more credence to the claims of positive therapeutic outcomes related to meditation and could lead to it becoming more widely used as a treatment among the mainstream medical community. We look forward to the results and what they can tell us about this ancient practice.

Besides the development of more scientific research, we have centuries of people noting the positive effect it has on their lives. Though we may not understand the mechanisms that underlie it, there are many tangible, positive benefits to the practice of meditation as people have sworn by its value for hundreds of years. People, who have practiced meditation for long periods, often report better handling stress and frustration, better concentration, can live in the moment, and more. It might be hard to quantify this in a scientific study, but it isn't hard for us to see how these things could be incredibly beneficial in daily life.

How to Meditate

The first thing you must do is find a clean, quiet place free from distractions. This might be a place in your house or even an outdoor location. You want privacy, so you aren't interrupted, and keep electronics out of the area unless you are using them for guided mediation or if you want to play soft, ambient music to help quiet outside noise you can't avoid and might cause distraction.

We cannot stress enough how important blocking out distraction is. If you cannot focus yourself on your practice, you will not get as much out of it as you could. It might be difficult for you to find a place in your home suitable for meditation, so consider outside areas. If you can get a few quiet minutes alone in your backyard or garden, this might be the best meditation spot for you.

You should be comfortable when you meditate. This includes the clothes you wear and how you sit. Most people wear loose, comfortable clothes. Meditation most often takes place seated on the floor, but you can sit on a pad or cushion to make this more comfortable. You don't have to wear exercise clothes; your everyday clothes will be fine. All that is required is that you wear something comfortable that won't distract you or make you uncomfortable during practice.

You want your body to be relaxed and comfortable, and not all of us can do the quintessential meditation pose for long periods of time, so it is a good thing it isn't necessary. The most important thing is to be comfortable and sit in a way that is conducive to deep breathing. You need to be able to take full, deep breaths, as this is a huge part of meditation. Most people meditate seated. You might sit on the floor, on a cushion, or even on a chair. There is no right way to meditate, except to get comfortable.

Before you meditate, you want to think about what you hope to get out of it. Are you looking for inner calm, a way to de-stress, or maybe personal insight? Whatever it is, you need to have your reasoning clear in your mind so you can state your intention and come up with a mantra, or short phrase, that relates to this intention. You will repeat this mantra later during practice.

Once you have stated your intention and know your mantra, close your eyes, and concentrate on your body. What do you feel? Focus closely on these sensations. Then, focus on your breathing. Take slow, dee breaths, focusing on breathing in and breathing out. This will help to focus your mind and relax your body. Do this for as long as you need to to feel yourself relax. This is when you know you are in the right frame of mind.

Once your breathing has become slow and deliberate, focus more closely on your breathing. Now, state your mantra and repeat it in your head. If you find yourself struggling, focus on something or a space in the room and don't take your eyes off it. The idea is to focus so closely on something that your mind becomes free of conscious thought, and you are living purely in the moment. It might take a few sessions for you to do this, but concentrating and focusing on an object or space can be helpful to get in this frame of mind.

Other Advice and Considerations

Though it might seem obvious, in order to get better at mediation, you must meditate! You must do it regularly and avoid taking long breaks between sessions. It will never get easier if you have a variable schedule of practice. You don't have to sit there staring at a wall for hours. Simply spending 10 minutes at a time, three to four times a week, is a great way to get started.

There is no benefit to overdoing it. It will probably lead to more negative issues than positive outcomes. There is also no need to spend hours on end trying to meditate. It isn't a marathon. Clearing your mind isn't something you can do for long durations when you aren't even used to doing it for short periods of time. You may have to try out different locations, using ambient music versus silence, using verbal mantras, or simply saying them in your head. We are all different, and what is most effective for you is what you should stick with. There is no *right way* to meditate.

Once you feel like you have mastered 10 minutes, kick it up to 20. There is really no need to practice for longer than this unless you want to. Some people will increase the number of times a week they practice, as they become more adepts at it.

You must have patience with meditation. As we stated earlier, it isn't easy and especially for those of us who live in urban areas. In the fast-paced Western world, clearing our minds and just sitting still for periods at a time isn't something we are conditioned to do. You are likely to have bad sessions where you can't concentrate or focus your mind. That's okay; you can try again.

If you continue to struggle in meditation, consider trying *guided practice*. This is generally led online, though it can be in person, by an expert at meditation who is there to guide you through the experience and keep you focused on what you need to be.

The great thing about meditation is that it helps to reduce stress and helps improve feelings of general wellbeing. It helps you pay more attention to life so you can appreciate and have gratitude for the little things. It can help you find ways to carve out your time, even in a hectic schedule. Meditation helps you be able to quiet your mind, and it can also make it easier for you to tune out negative thoughts that often cause self-doubt and other negative emotions. There is also evidence it helps to lower blood pressure, making it something that is good for our minds, bodies, and souls.

Regardless of the type of mediation you practice, where you practice, and how you practice it, there is a lot of evidence to support the positive benefits on our overall mental wellbeing. It can help us feel calmer and clearer in our thoughts and feelings. The act of meditation itself gives us a few minutes to take ourselves away from the hustle and bustle of the world and cut out a few moments where we can just be. Doing so can make us more easily able to manage stress or emotionally charged situations and can make it possible for us to unwind our minds, which so many of us need to do in today's stressful world.

It is worth the time and effort it takes to practice, and thankfully, this isn't an expensive practice to pick up. You need nothing except yourself and a cushion. You can easily find help sites online to give you tips on how to improve your meditation, how to get over common pitfalls and to give you mantras you can use in practice if you are studying. There are countless books and videos that will also help you understand the basics of practice.

You can often find guided meditation videos online for free and music carefully curated for use while meditating. Since many of us live in urban areas and don't have a good spot, we can get away from all the noise; having well selected ambient tracks available can be helpful.

Some people participate in group mediation or in-person mediation, and you might be surprised at just how many types of meditation there are. Mediation can be done alone; in groups, there are even walking meditation groups. To go a bit beyond just meditation, consider taking a yoga class in person or online to use meditation techniques in a stretching exercise routine that is also highly beneficial for your body and soul.

Try different types of meditation and practice it in different settings. Try music and try silence. Find what works for you. We are all different, and to get the full benefits of meditation, we must find what works best for us. When you notice that something you have tried has allowed for greater focus, or you feel like you got more out of a session, note it and integrate it into future sessions. You will eventually find a routine that works for you.

Chapter 11: Daily Affirmations

We have mentioned self-mantras and positive affirmations several times throughout this book, but now it is time to look closely at what this actually means and how we can put them into practice.

A positive affirmation is a short mantra or sentence we tell ourselves daily to help reduce stress and boost our self-esteem. It might seem silly, but there is a lot of benefit in giving little pep talks to tell ourselves it will all be okay, that we are worthy, and that we will make it through whatever the day may bring. Many people find this to be helpful, even those who were skeptical at first about the usefulness of positive affirmations.

Self-Affirmation Theory

Self-affirmation theory is a psychological theory that asserts that positive self-affirmation can help us boost our feelings of self-worth and make us feel like we have the potential to meet challenges and achieve goals. When we practice self-affirmation, it becomes part of our personal narrative.

MRI evidence indicates that parts of the brain, including the prefrontal cortex, become more active when we engage in self-affirmation. This part of the brain is associated with information about self and information processing. This indicates that our brain is internalizing these mantras and associating them with the self. Some also believe the self-affirmation can reduce stress.

When we practice self-affirmation, we become more prepared to manage emotionally charged situations and make us more like to practice self-care. Not only can these affirmations help improve our feelings of value and worth, but they can also give us a more generally positive outlook on life, which, in turn, makes us healthier mentally. Some psychologists also recommend the use of positive self-affirmation to get over trauma.

There is also a wealth of personal testimony about the effectiveness of daily positive self-affirmation. They can help put us in the right headspace to face our day with kindness and compassion, both towards others and ourselves. It might feel forced and not genuine at first, but this is common and natural. The more you do it, the more you can internalize what you are saying, and the more you will benefit from it. Many people do this as part of their morning routine to help prepare them for the day's stresses.

Examples of Daily Mantras

Now that we know some science behind the value of positive affirmation let's talk about how this is done and what types of phrases are used in these affirmations. One of the best ways to get the most out of daily affirmations is to use it as a short meditation session with the affirmation as your mantra.

Find a quiet, private place where you can be free of distractions and clear your head. Focus on your breathing, like you do during meditation, until you feel yourself physically relax, and your mind is clear of daily toils.

Next, you want to visualize a peaceful, quiet setting that is the epitome of calm for you. This should include detailed visualization. Think about the sounds, the sights, the smells, and focus on each one of these in turn. Not only will this make you feel good; it is a trick to get daily thoughts and worries out of your mind, so you are making your daily affirmations in a good mental space.

Creating this sense of inner calm helps you start the day more relaxed and may make it easier to internalize and really take to heart the affirmations you speak.

Now that you know what type of environment you need to say your daily affirmations in, let's look at some specific mantras you might choose for yourself.

Inner Health Studios Provides the Following Examples of Positive Affirmations

- I am at peace with myself
- I deserve to be happy
- My future is bright and positive
- I value myself as a person

Jessica DW Offers the Following Affirmations

- I am my best source of motivation
- Everything is possible
- I am compassionate with others and myself
- I appreciate all I have
- All I need is within me
- I attract positive people into my life
- I am stronger than I seem

Life Sorted Offers Mantras as Well Since Not All Mantras are Self-Directed, You Might Consider Ones Intended for Others

- You are powerful
- You should be proud of yourself
- I am limitless
- I love my flaws

- Believe in yourself

Positive Psychology Offers Slightly More Detailed Affirmations
- I believe in myself and trust my own wisdom
- My life is taking place right here, right now
- Nobody but me decides how I feel
- I am confident and capable of what I do

These are just a few examples. You can find countless more at various places online, and there are even books full of affirmations if you are struggling to find one that meets your exact needs. Don't just rely on these though, come up with your own that are personalized and meaningful to you. These phrases and statements can help you guard against negative thoughts that create excessive doubt and erode self-esteem. This should be done regularly, and many do it daily as a part of their self-care routine.

Chapter 12: Applying Self-Care

Self-care is something we have talked about numerous times throughout this book but haven't gone into the outside of a surface glance. Too many of us feel like doing anything good for ourselves is selfish and a luxury we shouldn't need, and this couldn't be farther from the truth. We can hardly live our best lives and offer anything to society if we are exhausted and mentally drained all the time. Nor can we feel great about ourselves if our diet is awful and hygiene is lacking.

Most people don't associate basic self-care with self-esteem, but they absolutely should. Failure to provide proper self-care is a symptom of low self-esteem, to begin with.

Self-care is multifaceted and goes beyond basic care for one's physical needs, though it does also include that. Self-care means care of the body, mind, and soul, not just the body. It isn't always easy to give ourselves the self-care we need since we are busy and pulled in many directions simultaneously. Most of us juggle many life roles: boss, coworker, friend, spouse, parent.

Some of us have been conditioned to think of self-care as selfish when it is vital to us being the best and offering the most to the world around us. What free time many of us do have is taken up by distraction rather than efforts to provide ourselves with the physical and mental nourishment we need.

But self-care shouldn't be something we even have to argue about; it should be obvious this is not only a good thing to do but also a vital thing to do. But we live in a society that sometimes has its priorities out of whack, and many of us believe that we are being selfish or could better use our time if we practice self-care.

Think about the people around you that need you: your family, your children, your coworkers, and your friends. If you cannot practice self-care for yourself, do it for them. They need you to be healthy and around for a long time, and if you continually fail to take care of your basic health and wellness, this might not be possible. We not only have a right, but we must take care of our minds and bodies not only for our own benefit but also to benefit those we love.

Ways to Improve Our Self-Care

There are a lot of ways we can improve our self-care, some more obvious than others. All are important, and while some of these things might not seem like that big of a deal, they are. When these are neglected over time, they can lead to health issues, psychological issues, and even more problems with self-esteem.

Though this might seem trite, sleep is incredibly important and vital for our physical and mental health. When we don't get enough sleep, we are more prone to illness, and we become less mentally prepared to handle stress, failure, and setbacks. Sleep really should be one of the prime focuses of any self-care routine.

We need to go to the doctor regularly to ensure that we are healthy and that no issues develop. This isn't necessarily easy as some people lack insurance or the financial means to obtain healthcare. If this applies to you, investigate community resources such as your local health department or any organizations dedicated to the health of its community members. This can put you in touch with low-cost or no-cost basic health services and may even provide access to low-cost mental health services.

We also must eat properly. The food we eat is the fuel our body uses to function and get us through our daily lives. Just like how putting bad fuel in a car makes it run less efficiently than it might otherwise, the same goes for us. We need to eat right, make sure we take time for important meals; that way, we aren't reaching for the chips while watching television in bed at night. As nice as it might seem, it isn't providing you with the fuel your body and mind need.

This can simply mean eating less sugar, making sure you are getting whole grains or cutting processed foods from your diet. These changes will have a significant positive impact on your health and improve your mental health and wellbeing.

Gut health is also important and something we don't give enough attention to. Helpful bacteria in the gut not only help aid in digestion, they aid in us getting the most nutrition out of our food, and there is evidence it can also contribute to our overall health. Getting healthy bacteria from your diet, such as by eating yogurt or drinking kombucha, is a great way to help keep your gut healthy.

We have all heard the adage about diet and exercise is the key component of health, and it is true. So now, we move on to exercise. You don't have to be a gym rat to get the benefits of exercise. Just a little activity like a short walk every day is more than enough. Keeping active helps keep you in shape and keep your internal organs operating optimally. And physical activity has been associated with reducing stress levels and aiding in sleep.

Now, we must move on to the less obvious parts of self-care. The first thing we need to address is our ability to say no. Most of us aren't flush with time, and the free time we have is valuable and should be used for things that enrich our lives. This is why we must learn how to say no and prioritize time for ourselves. It's helpful to block out personal time and be sure to stick to it.

Mostly, self-care should be enjoyable (exercise might be an exception here, but we still have to do it!) It helps to start with the basics and then move on to higher-order needs. When we have gotten enough sleep, practice good hygiene, and make time for ourselves, we are likely to find we feel better overall, and this makes us better equipped to handle the rigors of daily life.

We mentioned earlier that some people actually block out specific time for self-care and if it takes for that you to provide for your own needs and stick to it, you should do this. Self-care goes beyond things we need to do for ourselves and extends to things we should reserve the right to avoid and refuse. We must allow ourselves control over as many aspects of our life as we can, and while we can't avoid all frustrating interactions (nor should we), we do have a choice in which we face and which we don't.

Some people create a "no list" of things they won't participate in. It is okay to dig your heels in and refuse to participate in activities that aren't conducive to healthy self-esteem and positive interaction. There are some negative things we have no choice but to engage in, but you do not have to go to a dinner party that includes someone who always brings up negative topics and ruins the evening.

Being creative is a part of self-care that a lot of us neglect. You don't have to be a talented artist or musician to be creative. Listening to music, cooking, coloring, doing crafts, or even reading are all creative endeavors that engage your mind and provide you with a sense of enjoyment and wellbeing. These are not frivolous things; they are an integral part of a happy and healthy life. Humans are inherently creative beings, and a failure to address this part of our basic needs can make our lives less satisfying than they otherwise might be.

As we noted in the first chapter, distractions are not bad in and of themselves; try to find creative or fun distractions that give you a good way to pass the time or de-stress after a long day. Crafting or doing something mentally stimulating like a puzzle or a word game is a great way to unwind and still use your faculties. It isn't just mindless consumption.

The Internal Elements of Self-Care

As we have seen, self-care is a lot more than just making sure we get proper hydration. It also entails being more present and in the moment, which is what our creative endeavors and healthy distractions help to provide. We should also learn to pay closer attention to how we feel and about what we are thinking. This is part of the path to self-knowledge, self-awareness, and self-acceptance.

When we notice ourselves feeling something, especially something negative, we should take a pause and look at it deeper. Are our feelings warranted? Is it just the inner critic in our head with nothing better to do than make us feel bad about ourselves? Think about whether the sense of doubt or negative inner talk you are feeling is helpful to your current situation. If it is, pursue these thoughts. If it isn't, acknowledge that you felt that way and move on.

Psychologists recommend all these means of self-care to reduce stress, improve confidence, and raise overall feelings of general wellbeing. As we learn who we are and what we need, we can better plan personalized self-care routines that attend to our individual needs. We all are unique and require different things to live our best lives. Learning who we are and how to account for these varied needs is rewarding; it allows us to put our best self forward, which is better for the people around us.

Many people find it helpful to steal moments throughout the day for brief bouts of self-care. Taking a few minutes for positive affirmations or having a quick meditation session is a great way to keep our stress under control and make sure we are caring for ourselves. Self-care should mean allowing yourself the time and space to pursue the things you enjoy while also learning to love yourself.

Conclusion

Self-esteem is an important but complicated aspect of human life. Healthy self-esteem levels make it easier for someone to get what they want out of life and live a happy, healthy and fulfilled life, but this is far easier said than done since there are so many things that contribute to our feelings of personal value and worth. Plus, a high level of self-esteem is not necessarily a good thing in and of itself.

Like with mostly anything in life, balance and moderation are key. We want to have enough self-esteem that we value ourselves and can ask for the things we want and need, and take risks to make our lives better and more fulfilling. Conversely, we don't want so much self-esteem we come across as arrogant. That is an unattractive quality and not at all what we are looking to achieve.

We have a lot working against us when we are adults with low self-esteem. We often develop low self-esteem because of life experiences. Whether as a child or an adult, negative life experiences, and a lack of positive feedback can make us unsure of ourselves and doubt our value to the world. It is hard to get past life of bad experience, but with effort, self-reflection, self-compassion, and the ability to let go of the past, we can heal from these experiences and boost our self-esteem in the process.

Most of us barely know what self-esteem means and often misunderstand how to calculate the worth we place on ourselves. Our self-esteem refers to the value we give ourselves when compared to others, how worthy we feel we are of love and respect, the amount of confidence we have in our abilities, and more. Having low self-esteem can often mean we fear failure and risk so much we don't even bother trying; instead, we live a life dictated by fear and the whims of others. It is hard to be satisfied with this life.

There is a lot of work involved in developing healthy levels of self-esteem. First, we must learn about ourselves. We must understand whom we are, what we want, and what we need out of life. We must understand our emotions and take responsibility to form the impact our emotions and behavior have on our lives. Once we do this, we can see areas of our life where we can regain control and see the other elements we can improve so we can become the person we want to be.

Learning who we are can be a lifelong process. We are a mixture of thoughts and emotions, and many of us spend so much of our life on autopilot that we never really stop to ask ourselves why we feel the way we do or why we believe what we believe. But knowing this is important. It can help you learn how to best live a life based on your values and beliefs. It can also help you learn what you think, especially for those who have long had their opinions commanded by others. We might not always like what we see, but we must learn how to work on the aspects of ourselves we can control, how to forgive, and how to accept ourselves for the parts we cannot control. The path to healthy self-esteem requires a lot of forgiveness and letting go of the past. This applies to others, of course, but most importantly, *to us.*

We must do a lot more than take responsibility for our actions and figure out what we feel and why, we also must learn how to accept ourselves as we are. Yes, there are things we can control and change about ourselves, but there are other things we cannot change. Eventually, it is this that we must come to terms with if we want to love ourselves and let ourselves be loved. We must accept who and what we are and forgive ourselves for past mistakes, regrets, or roads not traveled.

Taking responsibility can be difficult and uncomfortable, but it is also empowering. It shows us there are many elements of our lives in which we can see a positive change because we have control over them. We must learn how to accept both the good and the bad, and that means we must take responsibility for the negative elements of our life we are responsible for. When we look closely at our lives, we will find areas of our lives and selves where we are abdicating responsibility onto someone else or some outside circumstance.

We must learn about distraction and why we choose it at certain times. Then, we must learn how to regain control over it so we are living life in the present and are actually "there" rather than on autopilot. A lot of what is entailed in improving our self-esteem is difficult, uncomfortable, and it takes time, but the effort is definitely worth it. Distraction keeps us from being present in our daily lives and can have a negative impact on our relationships when we aren't fully engaged with the world. Most of us do this without even knowing we are doing it; we do it mindlessly.

Distraction, like so much of what we talked about in this book, is not something to be avoided, but, we need to be more conscious of and in control. There is nothing inherently wrong with distraction, and it serves a really good purpose in allowing us moments of freedom from the rigors of life. That said, there must be a balance. We must allow ourselves distractions, but consciously so. We must know that we are using distractions and that we have a good reason for doing it.

A big part of gaining self-esteem is learning how to live in the present and becoming cognizant of what is going on around you. This will make it easier for you to read a situation and pick up nonverbal cues you might otherwise miss. Plus, it will mean you are actually present in your social interactions. It's hard to listen to your spouse tell a story about their day when you are also scrolling through social media at the same. It not only makes it hard to pay attention, but it also sends a clear message to your partner they are not getting your full attention, and that isn't something we should want them to feel.

A vital component of all of this is developing a positive level of assertiveness. This, of course, does not mean becoming overbearing and dominating, but, developing the ability to ask for what you need and make sure your opinion is heard. It involves you taking ownership of your feelings and learning to express them in positive ways. It isn't easy to develop self-assertiveness because many of us have a lifetime of letting others direct the ins and outs of our lives. Some of us also come from cultures where certain groups of people (like women) are not raised to be assertive, and it may even lead to negative consequences in their lives.

We also must step back and look at our social circle and think about who we are friends with and why. We need to make sure our support networks comprise people who you love and respect and who love and respect you. Sometimes becoming more confident will require you to reduce the influence certain people have over your life if they aren't affecting it in a positive way. As the name implies, a support network should offer you positive support in your time of need, as you should provide them the same in return. Relationships of all types should be mutually beneficial and not a competition.

It is also important to think about whom we compare ourselves to and why. This is why we have to look closely at our social media use and focus on celebrity culture. These things can be fun and harmless in small doses, but research shows that too much focus on these things has a negative effect on our feelings of value and worth. Remember, it is imperative we manage this so it either has a positive impact or no impact on our life.

When we realize that we are using social media in an unhealthy way (detrimental to our feelings of self-worth and value), we either need to adjust how we view and see social media or remove ourselves from it entirely. Few people will live a life without social media because it is a great way to keep up with friends and family and engage with others who share our interests. This is fine, but we must look closely at our usage to ensure this is actually what we are doing with our time on social media.

Though it might not seem like a huge deal, social media can have a profound impact on our lives and how we feel we stack up against other people. Thus, it is vitally important to find a healthy way to use social media, or you may have to withdraw from it for periods of time. Some people take "screen breaks" where they don't look at social media for a weekend here and there. This can be a great way to get your head out of that unrealistic virtual space and get yourself re-centered in the real world with more realistic expectations.

So much of developing our self-esteem requires us to learn and figure out how to control what we can accept and what we can't. It also requires us to develop confidence in our thoughts, feelings, and ideas so we can express them and act when necessary. One way we can help our confidence, and our lives, is to participate in something bigger than ourselves.

When we involve ourselves with a hobby, cause, or organization that goes beyond our own little existence, we find meaning and purpose in life that many think of as one of the defining features of human life. Not only will this help you live your life by your values, but it also takes away reasons for your inner critic to rear its ugly head and fill you with negative self-thought. It is also rewarding and a positive thing for the world.

Learning how to care for ourselves physically, mentally, and spiritually is something that we must work on for a lifetime. Finding ways to be more present and live a more mindful life helps us reduce stress, improve our sense of physical and mental wellbeing, and foster good health. Taking care of ourselves, whether by meditating regularly or making sure we get enough sleep, will go a long way towards helping us become better able to handle stress and negativity, which often work to better our self-esteem.

Taking care of oneself is not selfish. It is hard to love others openly and provide something of value to the world when we aren't even willing to properly defer our own basic life needs. Loving ourselves makes us better friends, partners, coworkers, and more.

All these things will take time, but the result will be worth it since the result is the ability to gain self-love and self-respect. Self-esteem is a varied and complex subject with a lot of variables that factor into how we feel about ourselves. If we want to improve our self-esteem, it will take a lot of work and conscious effort, but it is possible to allow ourselves love and forgiveness and to strive towards becoming that person we know we are inside.

Here's another book by Mark Jeffers that you might like

References

A Nice Person's Guide to Becoming Assertive. (2020). Mindforlife.Org. https://www.mindforlife.org/nice-persons-guide-becoming-assertive/

Ackerman, C. (2018, November 6). What is Self-Worth and How Do We Increase it? (Incl. 4 Worksheets). PositivePsychology.Com. https://positivepsychology.com/self-worth/

Ackerman, C. (2019, July 3). What is Self-Awareness and Why is it Important? [+5 Ways to Increase It]. PositivePsychology.Com. https://positivepsychology.com/self-awareness-matters-how-you-can-be-more-self-aware/

Assertiveness | Psychology Today. (2019). Psychology Today. https://www.psychologytoday.com/us/basics/assertiveness

Baratta, M. (2018). Self Care 101. Psychology Today. https://www.psychologytoday.com/us/blog/skinny-revisited/201805/self-care-101

Baumeister, R. F., Campbell, J. D., Krueger, J. I., & Vohs, K. D. (2003). Does High Self-Esteem Cause Better Performance, Interpersonal Success, Happiness, or Healthier Lifestyles?

Psychological Science in the Public Interest, 4(1), 1–44. https://journals.sagepub.com/doi/10.1111/1529-1006.01431

Beach, J. (2017, June 6). Why People Who Have a Life Purpose Have Higher Self-Esteem. Lifehack. https://www.lifehack.org/597693/why-people-who-have-a-life-purpose-have-higher-self-esteem

Boyes, A. (2018, June 19). 5 Self-Sabotaging Things Unconfident People Do. Psychology Today. https://www.psychologytoday.com/us/blog/in-practice/201806/5-self-sabotaging-things-unconfident-people-do

Brockway, J. (2019, December 9). The 31 Absolute Best Body Positivity Moments of 2019. Good Housekeeping; Good Housekeeping. https://www.goodhousekeeping.com/health/wellness/g28497513/body-positivity-moments-2019/

Brown, M. (2019, May 18). 9 Signs of Low Self-Esteem & 10 Ways Grow Confidence. The Couch: A Therapy & Mental Wellness Blog. https://blog.zencare.co/boost-self-esteem/

Bruening, L. (2019, October 19). Personal Responsibility and Mental Health. Psychology Today. https://www.psychologytoday.com/us/blog/your-neurochemical-self/201910/personal-responsibility-and-mental-health

Burgess, J. (2019, November 25). 21 powerful positive affirmations for confidence and self-esteem. Life Sorted. https://www.lifesorted.com/positive-affirmations-for-confidence/

Burton, N. (2012). Building Confidence and Self-Esteem. Psychology Today. https://www.psychologytoday.com/us/blog/hide-and-seek/201205/building-confidence-and-self-esteem

Caiola, R. (2016, October 25). 8 Ways To Practice Self-Acceptance. HuffPost. https://www.huffpost.com/entry/8-ways-to-practice-self-acceptance_b_12640812

Davis, T. (2018). Self-Care: 12 Ways to Take Better Care of Yourself. Psychology Today. https://www.psychologytoday.com/us/blog/click-here-happiness/201812/self-care-12-ways-take-better-care-yourself

Deep H, O. P. for. (2018, February 6). 7 skills of self-responsibility. Medium. https://medium.com/what-is-the-real-cause-of-depression/7-skills-of-self-responsibility-bb882edd506b

DW, J. (2018, April 13). 30 Affirmations for Confidence. Jessica DW | Spiritual Leadership Coach. https://jessicadw.com/blog/2018/4/13/30-affirmations-for-confidence

Eurich, T. (2018, April 23). What Self-Awareness Really Is (and How to Cultivate It). Harvard Business Review. https://hbr.org/2018/01/what-self-awareness-really-is-and-how-to-cultivate-it

Free Relaxation Script: Self-Esteem Relaxation. (n.d.). Www.Innerhealthstudio.Com. https://www.innerhealthstudio.com/self-esteem-relaxation.html

Friedman, W. J. (2015). Self-Responsibility/Self-Accountability Qualifies You as an Adult - Wellness, Disease Prevention, And Stress Reduction Information. Mentalhelp.Net. https://www.mentalhelp.net/blogs/self-responsibility-self-accountability-qualifies-you-as-an-adult/

Friendman, W. J. (2016, January 21). The importance of self-responsibility. Red Deer Advocate. https://www.reddeeradvocate.com/life/the-importance-of-self-responsibility/

Fuller, J. R. (2015, March 27). Social Media Use and Self-Esteem. New York Behavioral Health. https://newyorkbehavioralhealth.com/social-media-use-and-self-esteem/

Graf, S. (2020, September 17). How to Meditate for Self Discovery. WikiHow. https://www.wikihow.com/Meditate-for-Self-Discovery

Hill, J. (2019, December 11). What Is Self-Worth and How to Recognize Yours. Lifehack. https://www.lifehack.org/854916/what-is-self-worth

How to Be Assertive Asking for What You Want Firmly and Fairly. (2009). Mindtools.Com. https://www.mindtools.com/pages/article/Assertiveness.htm

How to Build Confidence Through Meditation | How to Beast. (n.d.). How to Beast. Retrieved from https://www.howtobeast.com/build-confidence-meditation/

How to Build Your Self-Worth When No One Taught You How. (n.d.). Tiffany Writes Things. Retrieved from https://www.tiffanywritesthings.com/personal-development/2018/11/1/how-to-build-your-self-worth-when-no-one-taught-you-how

https://www.facebook.com/FrankSonnenbergOnline. (2014, December 16). 7 Ways To Live Life With a Purpose. Frank Sonnenberg Online. https://www.franksonnenbergonline.com/blog/7-ways-to-live-life-with-a-purpose/

https://www.facebook.com/verywell. (2019). 5 Ways to Start Boosting Your Self-Confidence Today. Verywell Mind. https://www.verywellmind.com/how-to-boost-your-self-confidence-4163098

Improving Assertiveness Self-Help Resources - Information Sheets. (n.d.). Www.Cci.Health.Wa.Gov.Au.

https://www.cci.health.wa.gov.au/Resources/Looking-After-Yourself/Assertiveness

Maier, R. (2018). Self-Responsibility: Transformations. American Behavioral Scientist, 63(1), 27–42. https://journals.sagepub.com/doi/10.1177/0002764218816802

Manson, M. (2018, May 3). The Three Levels of... Mark Manson; Mark Manson. https://markmanson.net/self-awareness

Marie, K., & Williams, B. (2020). Self-awareness theory and decision theory: a theoretical and empirical integration. https://core.ac.uk/download/pdf/38917907.pdf

Mayo Clinic Staff. (2017). Stressed out? Be assertive. Mayo Clinic. https://www.mayoclinic.org/healthy-lifestyle/stress-management/in-depth/assertive/art-20044644

McCarthy, M. (n.d.). Why strong self-esteem is the secret to success in life. Www.Createwritenow.Com. https://www.createwritenow.com/journal-writing-blog/why-strong-self-esteem-is-the-secret-to-success-in-life

Meditation: In Depth. (n.d.). NCCIH. https://www.nccih.nih.gov/health/meditation-in-depth

Michael, R. (2018, July 8). What Self-Care Is — and What It Isn't. World of Psychology. https://psychcentral.com/blog/what-self-care-is-and-what-it-isnt-2/

Miller, K. D. (2020, January 7). Using Self-Awareness Theory and Skills in Psychology. PositivePsychology.Com. https://positivepsychology.com/self-awareness-theory-skills/

Moore, C. (2019, March 4). Positive Daily Affirmations: Is There Science Behind It? PositivePsychology.Com. https://positivepsychology.com/daily-affirmations/

Morin, A. (2017, July 11). How Do You Measure Your Self-Worth? Psychology Today. https://www.psychologytoday.com/us/blog/what-mentally-strong-people-dont-do/201707/how-do-you-measure-your-self-worth

Olatunbosun, M. (2018, November 7). 13 Ways Living with Purpose Makes You Happier and More Fulfilled. Lifehack. https://www.lifehack.org/814085/living-with-purpose

Pillay, S. (2016, May 16). Greater self-acceptance improves emotional well-being - Harvard Health Blog. Harvard Health Blog. https://www.health.harvard.edu/blog/greater-self-acceptance-improves-emotional-well-201605169546

Powell, A. (2018, April 9). Harvard researchers study how mindfulness may change the brain in depressed patients. Harvard Gazette; Harvard Gazette. https://news.harvard.edu/gazette/story/2018/04/harvard-researchers-study-how-mindfulness-may-change-the-brain-in-depressed-patients/

Raghunathan, R. (2011, December 14). Take Personal Responsibility, Don't Blame Others. Psychology Today. https://www.psychologytoday.com/us/blog/sapient-nature/201112/take-personal-responsibility-dont-blame-others

Ravenscraft, E. (2019, June 3). Practical Ways to Improve Your Confidence (and Why You Should). The New York Times. https://www.nytimes.com/2019/06/03/smarter-living/how-to-improve-self-confidence.html

Robins, R. W., & Trzesniewski, K. H. (2005). Self-Esteem Development Across the Lifespan. Current Directions in Psychological Science, 14(3), 158–162. https://journals.sagepub.com/doi/10.1111/j.0963-7214.2005.00353.x

Schwitzgebel, E. (2010). Introspection (Stanford Encyclopedia of Philosophy). Stanford.Edu. https://plato.stanford.edu/entries/introspection/

Self-Care. (n.d.). Active Minds. https://www.activeminds.org/about-mental-health/self-care/

Self-Esteem | Psychology Today. (2019). Psychology Today. https://www.psychologytoday.com/us/basics/self-esteem

Setlzer, L. (2011). The Path to Unconditional Self-Acceptance. Psychology Today. https://www.psychologytoday.com/us/blog/evolution-the-self/200809/the-path-unconditional-self-acceptance

Smith, J., Suttie, J., Jazaieri, H., & Newman, K. (2018, November 12). 10 Things We Know About the Science of Meditation - Mindful. Mindful. https://www.mindful.org/10-things-we-know-about-the-science-of-meditation/

Sokal, J. (2011, August 30). What You Need to Live a Life of Purpose. Tiny Buddha. https://tinybuddha.com/blog/what-you-need-to-live-a-life-of-purpose/

Tartakovsky, M., & read, M. S. L. updated: 8 O. 2018 ~ 4 min. (2016, May 17). Therapists Spill: 12 Ways to Accept Yourself. Psychcentral.Com. https://psychcentral.com/lib/therapists-spill-12-ways-to-accept-yourself/

Taylor, J. (2010, June 7). Popular Culture: America's Self-esteem Problem. Psychology Today. https://www.psychologytoday.com/us/blog/the-power-prime/201006/popular-culture-americas-self-esteem-problem

The Importance of Self-Worth - PsychAlive. (2014, May 9). PsychAlive. https://www.psychalive.org/self-worth/

Tucker-Ladd, C. (2010, February 25). Building Assertiveness in 4 Steps. World of Psychology. https://psychcentral.com/blog/building-assertiveness-in-4-steps/

Why Self-Esteem is Important and Its Dimensions. (2015). Mentalhelp.Net. https://www.mentalhelp.net/self-esteem/why-its-important/

Wignall, N. (2019, March 15). Assertiveness: A Step-by-Step Guide to Becoming More Assertive [2020]. Nick Wignall. https://nickwignall.com/assertiveness/

www.ingramcontent.com/pod-product-compliance
Lightning Source LLC
LaVergne TN
LVHW041645060526
838200LV00040B/1722